The
Beauty
of Gesture

The Beauty of Gesture

*The Invisible
Keyboard
of Piano
and T'ai Chi*

Catherine David

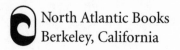 North Atlantic Books
Berkeley, California

The Beauty of Gesture
The Invisible Keyboard of Piano and T'ai Chi

North Atlantic Books
P.O. Box 12327
Berkeley, California 94712

Distributed to the book trade by Publishers Group West

Cover and book design by Paula Morrison

The Beauty of Gesture: The Invisible Keyboard of Piano and T'ai Chi is sponsored by the Society for the Study of Native Arts and Sciences, a nonprofit educational corporation whose goals are to develop an educational and crosscultural perspective linking various scientific, social, and artistic fields; to nurture a holistic view of the arts, sciences, humanities, and healing; and to publish and distribute literature on the relationship of mind, body, and nature.

Library of Congress Cataloguing-in-Publication data

David, Catherine.
    [Beauté du geste. English]
    The beauty of gesture : the invisible keyboard of piano
& t'ai chi / Catherine David ; translated by the author.
        p.   cm.
    Includes bibliographical references (p.   )
    ISBN 1-55643-219-4 (pbk.)
    1. Music—Philosophy and aesthetics.   2. Piano—
Performance.   3. T'ai chi ch'üan. I Title.
ML3849.D3813   1996
781.1'7—dc20   95-52654
                                                    CIP
                                                    MN

Contents

*To the residents and regulars
of the rue du Pré aux Clercs*

To the memory of my father

Foreword

My hope is to communicate a double personal experience: the steady and parallel practice of playing the piano and of t'ai chi ch'uan. Over the years I have discovered, through the minutest details, their surprising and hidden similarities.

The art of piano playing could be defined as an attempt to *touch music.* T'ai chi ch'uan, a specific practice of the Chinese martial arts, may be defined as a strategy to *touch the opponent.* (In Cyrano de Bergerac's words: "The poem ends, and I touch!" He comments on this verse by aiming his sword at his rival, making it clear that "I touch" refers not only to the fatal thrust of the weapon, but also to the act of writing.) At a given time, the art of fighting *(like the art of love),* calls for total commitment in one's relationship with the other person, opponent or partner.

Although efficiency remains the ultimate test in any martial art, it is a more intimate aspect, the "musical" experience of t'ai chi ch'uan, which I will try to share here. From this inner perspective, only the sensation aroused by motion sets the tone. If the sensation is coherent, the thrust of the sword will touch, the arrow will strike home, the music will come alive.

The aim is not to solve the mystery, but to unravel it and learn from it.

The
Beauty
of Gesture

"In the right foot, a first step is waiting."

Rainer Maria Rilke,
Description of *L'Homme des premiers âges*
by Auguste Rodin

I

Playing the piano is not a martial art. Very few pianists are concerned by the subtleties of attack and parry. And even fewer master swordsmen play Chopin.

Yet pianists and students of the martial arts would have much to say to each other. The beauty of gesture is their common interest, the focus of their effort, the means of their art, and perhaps its ultimate goal. It is impossible to separate it from the sensation it gives, the efficiency it ensures.

Pianists and practitioners of t'ai chi ch'uan invariably experience this: motion becomes more demanding as perceptions sharpen. The difference is the same as that between the wish to travel and the actual departure. Only patient repetition confers finesse and scope to a specific gesture, just as brushstrokes to and fro across a canvas enhance the colors. According to the monk and painter Shitao, "Bitter-Pumpkin," "no matter how far you go, how high you climb, you must begin with a single step."[1]

Repetition is not monotonous; it simply does not exist. "I love you more today than yesterday, and much less than tomorrow." One cannot bathe twice in the same river; if they are alive, two gestures can never be exactly alike even if they succeed each other in the blink of an eye. Likewise, two performances of the same sonata or the same stage play, two fights, two chess games, two loving embraces are never exactly the same.

What might seem an ordeal, then, is really an adventure, a moving landscape. Along the way, one discovers that strength and subtlety, agility and softness, speed and patience are complementary pairs: the most difficult is not always the most dramatic. Cognoscenti also say that authentic freedom stems from respecting the form.

The secret of these travelers? The joy of the quest. The perfect gesture is a Grail waiting in the depths of the future, at the edge of possibility. It recedes as one comes closer, like a mirage vanishing on the horizon, only to shimmer again farther away, ever more beautiful and enthralling.

This is a conspicuous mystery, undermining language, foreign to words and thoughts, careless as truth may be. Any attempt to transcribe the obvious tends immediately to deny it, flatten it, lose it. But perhaps one may also catch it in a glimpse, peep under its robe, unveil it, turn it into an offering.

Professionals have little need for words. When one is deeply committed to a single path, experience makes sense on its own. But to amateurs like myself, forever banished from the hinterlands of the continents whose shores they roam, language may serve as a map to hidden treasures: archi-pelagos, latitudes, ancient forests. Sentences serve as makeshift boats heading upriver. Is not writing, as well as t'ai chi ch'uan[2] and piano playing, an experience of the limits of language?

Air from the open sea rushed into the river's folds, under the generous hip of the bridge. You leaned toward me, but the film was playing in slow motion

*and you never finished not kissing me. Longing
was aroused like a call for air in the suspended
gesture ...*

In its search for the accurate form, writing is
akin to the gesture. It does not call upon conscious
thought alone to build its center, although
conscious thought is necessary every time one
uses words. But the "labor" of poetry is a process
of growth, a gestation, not something that happens
in a factory.

The word is to the idea what the gesture is to
the sensation—its physical manifestation. Ideas
don't exist outside of words, nor do sensations
outside the body. The word is both an incarnation
of the idea and the artisan of its conception; the
gesture is both the expression of the sensation
and its cause. The idea is the vibration of the word,
its resonance, its genealogy, its hidden side; the
sensation is the atmosphere of the gesture, its
invisible reality.

Despite these suggestive analogies, we all know
that the map is not the terrain; the written word
can only betray motion, the way it betrays music.
Slow, analytical, it is too focused upon its own
logic not to lose most of the fish it tries to catch.
From the living gesture to the words pinned to
the page, a part of reality gets lost, perhaps its
essential part. (The water in the river, for instance?)
However, in this game the loser wins—or so I'm
prepared to wager. Effort is the pride of desire.

II

Nor is piano playing a sexy game. At most, a play of fingers, hands, arms, shoulders, a sensual initiation devoted to the divinity of sound. It does not compare with long, warm, spiraling bodies improvising love. Unlike the pianist, whose freedom is determined by his faithfulness to the written score, lovers have genius as long as they improvise. But sometimes the piano surrenders to motion just as time surrenders to love.

No possible analogy then, or so it seems, between the gestures of love (flickers of the absolute illuminating the weave of days) and the repetitive gestures of a pianist scaling a Chopin *Étude.* Ten times the rocky path of this arpeggio, twenty times the suspended bridge of this stubborn crescendo, a hundred times this phrasing, this somersault, this scale in thirds, this ascension. And start over again tomorrow, day after day, iron out the kinks, stitch up the transitions, oil the gears. Lighten the wrists, stabilize the contrasts, weigh the sounds by becoming sensitive to the "escape," that tiny pause the finger senses while pressing down the key. And most of all, seek the mysterious "depth of the keyboard" which teachers are always talking about and which modulates the weight of the hammer on the string, whatever the intensity of the sound.

The supreme difficulty is to retain this deep contact with the keyboard while playing pianissimo, at the confines of silence and sound (Debussy's

Voiles). It feels like squaring a circle, blending weight and grace (Botticelli); but if the pianist fails to resolve this contradiction, he remains forever estranged from his art. To musicians, pianissimo represents the same challenge as extreme slowness to the student of t'ai chi ch'uan. In playing the piano as in practicing martial arts, technical skill maliciously requires that impossible tasks be converted into simple ones, that obstacles become springboards. In other words, constant mutation of pain into pleasure. Nothing less.

The essence of technical skill is the "double bind," ennobled into pedagogy: the impossible command. In the ideal of the Zen archer, is not the "want without wanting, shoot without shoot-ing" the only adequate aim? And is there not, in the high tension of love, the same mixture of "yes" and "no," resistance demanding defeat, and the desire to be endlessly reinvented?

"Be strong without clenching your muscles; bring your knee forward and your hip backward; push and pull at the same time; be conscious of the connection between feet and skull, hands and knees; let your fingers, your arms, rise slowly toward the ceiling as if pulled up by reverse gravity; combine flexibility and power, slowness and speed...." "Impossible!" moans the beginner whose thumb stalls in the middle of an arpeggio. "My legs are aching!" begs the student of t'ai chi ch'uan after a quarter-hour of standing exercises with knees bent.

True technical skill, as demonstrated by a great artist, brings forth the cry: How simple it looks!

Sensitive and sensual, it never produces the nightmarish scales that drive the neighbors crazy. Being a system of contradictory tensions, it endows gestures with density. In fact, technical skill is alone in charge, provided one understands its broadest meaning, which never separates agility from expression. Its mission is to remind us of the difficulty of what seems easy, and to make easy what seems difficult.

Technical skill is the core of what my dear maestro André Boucourechliev calls the "No, no, no ... *yes!*" This is one of the great secrets of musical expression. "No, no, no, I won't play that E-flat ... ah yes, I yield!" At last I play it, I hear it! *(At last we kiss!)* Technical, also, is the suspense, the longing created by this slight delay (unmeasured by the metronome), and the emotion it brings out. "All is technique!" says Boucourechliev, quoting his master Gieseking.

So it happens that, struggling along, one reaches a miraculous, fleeting moment of grace. (That there may be more than one in the course of a lifetime should make us weak with gratitude.) Each one of these brings a discovery, a new land-scape. A few bars of paradise foster the fusion of opposites, the heightening of possibles, the unity of breath. The exhilaration is too strong, then, to remain unnoticed but vanishes at the first inkling of intimate pride, and the pianist's hands empty as she takes refuge in old habits which now feel awkward, frail, irritating.

Still, you have a fresh nugget in your bag. And you go for more, scaling the heights at the tip of your fingers, riding roller-coasters, falling into traps.... Later comes the time when you reach a point of saturation: the score feels too familiar and further progress seems stalled. No matter how hard you try, fuzzy passages still resist every effort. In desperation, you push the piece aside and lock it away in the caves of your pianistic memory where other ancient pieces in dubious condition are stored. Let it mature. Six months later, you surrender and return to it: "This time I'll tame it for good!" Illusory hope: from the first bars, everything is out of shape. Can do better. Start from scratch. Rebuild. As technical skill improves, more numerous and exacting demands arise. Music doesn't come in a gift parcel; it is the mirage of the quest. Seeking for the nuance is what gives meaning to the effort. That this ordeal may be pleasurable—that is the surprise.

III

Down on our knees in the hazy morning,
lined up like penguins awaiting the tide, forehead
an inch from the floor, arms stretched forward,
hands flat on the ground, thumbs and index
fingers joined, we salute the divinity of the present.
A subtle ritual takes hold of us. Barely awake,
rivals in solidarity, we are brought together by
time, place, effort. An intimate Orient flows in
our veins.

It is the body's very substance that the
sensation sets out to explore. Relax your back,
stretch your toes, be aware of your breath, sense
the rush of blood in your skull, the weight and
heat in your eyeballs, the supple expanse of your
tongue, the curve of your spine. Dismiss last
night's dream, that intruder. Watch your insides,
viscera, muscles, circulating fluids. Push your
breath through your bones. Make a note of
sensitive spots, sluggish areas, lack of symmetry.
Feel the softness of the air on your skin, the
weight of your clothes.

Become conscious of the fact not of *having* a
body, but of *being* your body, this very minute:
belly, heart, lungs, muscles.... Where are the
limits between each of these "things"? Where
does the wrist end, the forearm begin? *(Mom, are
my ears part of my neck or not?)* Where lies the
border between belly and chest, between pelvis
and back? Gradually, words begin to lose their
usual meaning. They heat up, as if in a forge, and
the fusion transforms them. Stand, move,

advance, relax, bounce, push, pull, turn, bend.
Alchemy of language, kindled by the gesture.

For years we have practiced, without giving it
much thought, a simple rotation of the knees in
horizontal circles, feet joined, palms flat on
kneecaps. One day, our Japanese teacher points
out that in this exercise, the ankles are as important
as the knees. This simple thought confers an
additional reality to the presence of the ankles,
which in turn makes us more aware of all the
other parts of the body silently participating in
the exercise. The link between knees and ankles
serves as a reminder of the link between wrists
and elbows. The center of gravity shifts to consolidate the position of the ankles in relation to the
feet, which changes the axis of the pelvis, the
slant of the spine, the tension of the shoulders....

Small causes, far-reaching effects. A butterfly's
wing brushing the Empire State Building may
cause a snowstorm in Siberia. In t'ai chi ch'uan,
as elsewhere, the essence rests in details.

IV

In J. S. Bach's *Fantasia in G minor* for organ,
transcribed for the piano by Franz Liszt, the
opening chord evokes an embrace, preceded by
flight. The spreading arms, propped against the
slopes of the air, expand the back, freeing the
chest. The elbows are curved, rounded, light, but
the shoulders remain low and elastic. The hands,
wide open (the claws of an eagle), glide slowly
over the geometry of the keys. The shape of the
fingers already holds the coming chord. Above
the pedal the right foot is waiting, propped on its
heel.

When all is ready, the eagle goes for a dive.
Or perhaps it is the keyboard that ascends toward
the tips of the fingers, as a landing strip unfurls to
meet an airplane. Their encounter gives birth to
the chord, but the surge of the sound is always a
surprise—pleasurable or disappointing!

If the descent is hurried—if the fingers are
tense, the wrists stiff, the back narrowed, the mind
blurred—the notes are scattered, they trip and
tumble. The chord is reduced to a juxtaposition
of notes (the sum is reduced to the addition of its
parts). When the gesture is broken, the sound is
warped, and the muscles are disappointed. *(As
thoughtless kisses deceive and hurt.)*

If the curve of the arm is right, the elbows free,
the breathing relaxed; if the fingers penetrate
deeply and simultaneously into the keyboard as
if into dough, then accuracy and sensuality blend
and music appears as an emanation, an aspect of

the beauty of the gesture. From the pianist's perspective, we can say neither that the music is the aim of the gesture, nor the reverse. Sound and gesture are contemporary, identical, undistinguishable. A subtle increase of weight poured through the fingertips establishes the bass note and creates a starting point from which the melody rises. The roots and the sky.

From then on, linked to its own past and future, the gesture fills up with music and becomes rounded, like the universe. It bounces forward and endures, while its mobile shape creates a spatial counterpoint to the invisible keyboard of sound. The beauty of the gesture renders time visible.

V

In the *dojo*,[3] one November morning. Here we are, every Monday and Wednesday morning at nine, assiduous despite traffic jams, aches and pains, hangovers, urges to slip back into bed and sleep until noon. Ten years ago I would have laughed if anyone had predicted I would eventually commit myself to such a discipline. I am not a lover of habits. Regular schedules bore me, as do meals at set times. Clock-driven time feels like an ill-fitting corset. But in this case, regular attendance is one conquest among many. We don't even dream of skipping class anymore, and we even arrive ten minutes early.

There is a stale smell, a mixture of dried sweat and waxed floors. Someone opens the fanlight. The light of day, filtered through the blinds, is not yet the icy whiteness of winter mornings; it slides on the floorboards like a reflection of the moon on a lake. So must the spirit of the warrior be. *(I think of a long streak of light on the black surface of the ocean. The reflection of the moon is undisturbed by the lapping of the waves. A mother cries out for her children, kidnapped by bandits. Her call, repeated like that of a lost bird, is heard clear through the sensitive universe. In the silver beam a rowboat, finely calligraphed by the evening light, advances without moving.)*

In the cobbled courtyard of the old building, a dog barks furiously. Taking off one's socks is tough. Then meeting the cool floor with flattened soles. Unfolding the rusty body in the blurry morning.

Relaxing the articulations. Softening the shoulders. Feeling, underneath the sleepy flesh, the solid resistance of gravity.

After the greeting ceremony, in itself a physical preparation, Kenji Tokitsu murmurs, *"Ri tsu zen!"*[4] The torture begins anew. Never once, in over a year, has he let us off. We ready ourselves to cross the desert. Memory plays no part in this ordeal, which consists of standing still, feet slightly apart, knees bent, back straight, head high. Nothing *outstanding*, nothing really awful, especially if the knees are only slightly bent. The arms, however, ascend and trace a magic circle in front of the chest.

Soon the heart begins to thump and the shoulders tense up. Warning! Relax those shoulders! Slow your breathing! Of course, this is most arduous, just the reverse of what one instinctively does during an effort. Step by step, peace returns, the shoulders let go a few inches and immediately the arms feel lighter; the strength required to hold them up is drawn straight from the belly. Muscles have almost nothing to do with it. The entire structure stems from the center. The hands open up, resting on the air. The back expands, the legs seem to dig into the floor, as if taking root.

"Imagine your silhouette reflected on the earth, beneath your feet." Obedient, we try to picture this ghostly double, a little fellow clinging to the soles of our feet, his head pointing to the antipodes. The banal idea that the earth is round now seems astonishing. Our soles become palms, ultrasensitive to the coolness of the wood, to the fleeting feeling of existing here and now. Leg-shaped roots grow beneath our feet, forging their way downward into our dreamy minds. Our hands, palms turned down, connect like magnets as they weigh the ever-thickening air. *(Where does the sky begin, did you ask?)* The chest sinks in slightly, causing no alteration in the angle of the thigh and the groin. The light wrist fosters the flow leading from the forearm to the hand. The fingers warm up. . . .

The wrist must be flexible and light, or, even better, *conductive*, whether in t'ai chi, piano-playing — or in the art of painting as described by Shitao: "If one does not paint with a free wrist, there will be flaws in the painting, and these flaws will in turn cause the wrist to lose its ease of inspiration." The free wrist, for the painter, requires that the hand be raised and rest on nothing but space itself. "Varying positions of the wrist allow for carefree natural effects; its transformations foster the unexpected, the bizarre; its eccentricity works miracles, and when the wrist is animated by the spirit, rivers and mountains offer their soul." The wrist is the last articulation through which the energy circulates on its way from the center of the body to the fist or the finger. The last bottleneck.

Even if the sensations manage to find their way from the toes to the forehead, a stiff wrist is enough to create a block and destroy the harmony of the gesture. Free the wrist and the flow is complete: every part of the body moves in unison, like a bag filled with heavy, warm water. Nor is this flow limited by the skin: the air too has become liquid, and the flowing sensation extends into the space kept empty by the span of the hands.

Settling in the posture is no easy task. Constant checking must be done, millimeter-small adjustments made: raise the elbows, deepen the bend of the knees, check the distance between the feet, their symmetry, relax the shoulders again, relax them even more, widen the back, lengthen the neck—all of this under the watchful eye of one's center of gravity, stable as a rock in the midst of an angry sea.

These incessant rectifications turn immobility into a promised land. Stillness is to the martial arts what silence is to music: spirited, alive, vibrant with echoes, full of possible gestures, potential melodies. Pounding. Breathing. The silence of the dojo is crowded with the sound of breathing, bird-song, muffled sighs, barks, gurgling pipes. The longer we remain motionless, the more agitated our insides become. Hearts pound, the muscles protest, each area of the body rebels in its own way.

Warmth flows into us. Bound together, enemies yet still comrades before the firing squad, we feel united in a sort of resigned stoicism which makes us persevere. Five, ten, fifteen minutes. He doesn't move. Neither do we. How far does he intend to take us? Beware of glancing at the clock in hopes of witnessing the leap of the minute hand! Time has stopped.

"All of a sudden, out of nowhere, moods, feelings, wishes, and worries pour forth, mingling incoherently," writes Eugen Herrigel.[5] Is there a way out, a way to take off, to forget where I am,

to avoid the challenge? Any excuse will do:
a phone call to make, errands to plan, the geraniums
(they need fertilizer), *your kiss yesterday morning*,
the IRS. There are plenty of wayward thoughts at
hand even here, out of the corner of one's eye.
"How interesting, C. has kept her socks on again,
she might slip, wouldn't that be fun?" Everyone
else is barefoot, a bunch of hairy toes. "This new
girl still has not understood the position of the
right foot. It's no big deal to bring in your toes a
bit more...."

Vagrant thoughts. Sniffle, blow your nose,
tug at your T-shirt, toss back a loose strand of
hair, watch your fellow sufferers. Each gap in
your concentration becomes an event, opens a
trap filled with dreams. Thoughts bleed out
before they revert to silence, that growing child.
Still motionless in the austere clarity of the
morning light, we stand there, cross canyons,
climb peaks, monitor our organs, permeated all
the while by the incessant melody of breath.
Gradually, the air gains consistency; later, in this
slowed-down atmosphere, postures will emerge
from this fixed stand into an orderly continuum.
At last we will be allowed to change stillness into
slowness, to transfer the accumulated energy
during the long wait into gestures.

Odors. Sweat. General inspection. Draw the
plexus slightly further back, search for the center.
Invisible yet sovereign, the center of gravity is the
foundation of the gesture. Akin to a mobile base,
it allows one to remain in a state of perpetual
imbalance—that is, to dance. I consciously fill

the space enclosed by my circled arms; my hands rise slightly to the level of my face. ("Never forget to protect the face!") This technical adjustment brings forth a new sensation: the magic circle expands in front of the chest as if there actually were a huge beach ball there that I could hug. I distinctly sense the rough damp plastic; I almost feel grains of sand rubbing against my skin. Months, years may go by until the beach ball appears.

Mental images are imaginary, but their effects are real. First window, first clue. As Shitao puts it: "A journey of one thousand leagues begins at your feet." The beach ball is only a humble start, heralding unknown thoughts and landscapes, unsuspected strengths. After a long, perilous voyage, Columbus' lookout sighted the tip of a peninsula, a shadow on the horizon. Subsequent exploration revealed the truth of what was in that moment only a spot on the traveler's retina: a continent.

The new world heralded by the sensation of the beach ball is an inner world, contained within ourselves. But it is as unexplored as the "New World" was to those wandering Europeans. Was it already there before it appeared through the sensation, this material abstraction? That is the question: how to "recognize" an unknown land, a never-before-felt feeling?

Students of the martial arts learn how to call upon an intimate part of their being, to which Westerners are usually blind. However, as soon as we experience the reality and power of the *tanden*— that source of energy rooted deep in the belly, between navel and groin, we "recognize" it. A new experience is given to us, a strange plenitude, familiar like a déjà vu. Calves, chest, shoulders, face—each part of the body participates in this impetus toward unity.

I warm up, weigh down, settle. This is the meeting point with myself. I recognize the landscape, the vegetation, the colors. Yet I have never before visited this country. It is no small paradox, this memory that links our inner selves to ancient Chinese masters.[6] Puzzling. How could we not marvel at the idea of repeating the gestures and, what's more, experiencing the same inner sensations as mythical fifteenth-century warriors, living an ascetic life in an isolated monastery? That such an encounter may be possible implies some kind of universal link between spirit and body. If we manage (on good days, in our imperfect manner) to experience the tanden as a center controlling our own body, if we can "recognize" this reality as being ours, it means that we must hold something in common with the Chinese monks (and the Holy Family), something that transcends historical differences. A kind of memory perhaps, silent and secret, untouched by civilization, indifferent frontiers of time and space. A memory foreign to words, yet fully human, for it opens the path towards creation.

Imitating the teacher in the dojo is already remembering something one isn't aware of knowing. "We conceive a memory just as we conceive an idea or a child," writes Henri Atlan of

Jewish ritual. "What happens, in fact, is that we give life to a memory, which does not mean that we bring it alive again, but that we conceive it and give birth to it, fertilize it, to make it grow a sprout."[7] Active memory comes from the future; it is selected, like the fertilized egg, from an infinite number of possibilities.

Suddenly, something vibrates in unison: flexibility, strength, impetus, memory. The frontier between stillness and motion, between ri tsu zen and a sequence of t'ai chi ch'uan gestures, blurs to the point of becoming impalpable, like a train's slow departure or the fading of twilight. Nothing is more surprising at first than this embodiment of thought in a sensation, this mutation of a mental image into solid flesh.

Matter starts to dream. The beach ball is all the more present for its absence. The air thickens, the empty space fills up. The atmosphere is so thick that movement becomes almost unthinkable. It would be enough, one feels, to *let go,* to let the beach ball fall, for the gesture to appear. The punch, the parry, would then be nothing else, at their best, than a release (under control—that is the challenge) of the inner thrust, a flame darting from the embers. There is something frightening about this excess of reality created by the mind's concentration and the body's compliance. As soon as one becomes aware of it, one tends to pull away, to forget it, to deny it. I vaguely wonder: Isn't this crazy? What am I doing in this torture room?

It isn't only the physical effort one tries to

escape from, but also the mental effort, the task of excluding peripheral thoughts. In t'ai chi ch'uan, the work of the mind is inseparable from the active body. From this perspective, the dismal exercise of jogging on a moving walkway, gaze riveted on a television screen, seems absurd. The temptation to flee from the new sensation primarily comes from its weird, troublesome, disturbing novelty, but also from the watchfulness it requires, the inner mobilization. Control of the gesture implies control of thoughts, an interruption of the inner monologue which we so often confuse with our identity, forgetting the revelation of silence.

There are days, I confess, when the appearance of the beach ball far from compensates for the efforts involved in standing there doing nothing when it would be so much nicer to stretch out and read, take a bath, or play the piano. (The piano also brings pain, but in a different, less physical way, through the quality of emotion it requires.) Any excuse will do to flee from this torture. Yet one comes back to it, out of necessity, as to a house in the darkness.

Awareness of the sensation is in fact the only way to dismiss boredom and convert muscular pain into pleasure. During one of these endless ri tsu zen sessions—unless one simply gives up, which would be humiliating—one has no other choice than to play along: welcome the beach ball and its material power. Give birth to this illusion, the damp grains of sand, the elastic roundness, the coolness, the friendly bulk. Immediately, the arms round up more gracefully, the hands feel strong without tensing up, the fingers feel free, the wrist follows the forearm, the legs consolidate one's stance, the body turns into a silent piano.

In the distance, beyond the boulevard, we hear the bells of Saint Thomas d'Aquin. Their ring has the heavy, majestic timber of bass voices in Mozart, scattering high pitched overtones. I raise my arms slightly. *A bird is singing. I have always known this bird. I used to hear it as a child, from the second floor window. It is still there, faithfully chirping, just at the right moment, in the strip of sky where time listens to the trees. The same bird, now I'm sure.* For the last few days, an early spring has been spreading an undeserved grace over Paris. The bird shakes the crystal of time and a pang of euphoria flits through me. Fervent memories surge within the present.

The floor displays its quiet geometry. The soles of our feet sink into the shining wood, digging in. The surface of the floor comes alive. Our sensations are no longer limited to our bodies; they now spread into the space between us and our companions, then through the entire dojo. The floor becomes a mirror: head hanging down toward the center of the earth (the center, again!), our twin suspended from our soles reflects an infinite. Vertigo.

VI

I don't know where I am headed, but already
the landscape has changed; the mountain is no
longer a blue haze. Colorado is split from north
to south along a perfectly vertical line: on the
right, the dreary, endless, sinister Midwest plains;
on the left, the superb mass of the Rocky
Mountains. Vision travels far across the flat
wilderness surrounding Denver. The mountain
can be seen from everywhere. But from here it is
only a shadow mountain, an immense blue haze
with a fuzzy outline; the earth, lazy beauty, is
raising her head, and her hair is a cascade of light.

The Rocky Mountains haunt the dreams of the
valley dwellers. I spent many evenings, as a child,
on the back porch of the Shriver home, watching
the majestic shape dissolve on the horizon as the
silent stars lit up. I didn't know, at the time, that
the soft blue color was an illusion.

One day we went by car on a picnic to the
"Rockies." I pictured large ladies carved in rock,
wearing hats. My grandpa drove his Plymouth
with respectful veneration, whistling constantly.
It was his way of purring. I have never since heard
anyone whistle like he did, from inside the mouth.
He hardly gave it any thought. Lips slightly apart,
he modulated the passing air between his palate
and his tongue, curled up sideways like a tulip
petal. The sound was tiny, almost inaudible. I
have inherited his gift and passed it on to my
daughter. One can whistle any tune this way.

Our Plymouth was green with slightly rusty

bumpers. It could easily seat four people in the front. On the dashboard stood a spherical compass with a trembling needle: in this geometrical land, even short trips have their direction. So we started up the highway and headed straight for the blue haze. I was prepared to touch the mountain, to wallow in the blue. I held my breath as we sped past the McDonalds *(6 billion served!)*, liquor stores, and gas stations.

I had been disappointed on the plane from Paris; we had climbed so high, so fast, that I thought we would bump into the sky. But the sky wasn't there to meet us, only air was there. The sky remained higher still, unattainable, and the blue stretched over us like a dome, a cloak of infinity draped around the earth.

Soon the road began to wind upward. Down below, a transparent river splashed over its pebble carpeting. Barely more visible than the air, the water sparkled tiny points of light. From the other side of the road, fir trees leaned their heavy branches toward us.

But where was the blue haze? Where were the Rocky ladies? I saw nothing but tons of earth-crust shaped by the fire of hell, and in the midst of this geological chaos, crystal waterfalls, wild-flowers, chipmunks. Altitude induces a euphoria exalted by the limpid scarcity of air. Near the old gold mines, steam engine trains, packed with children and popcorn-eating tourists, brayed around the slopes of the foothills.

To my great surprise I realized I was there. We were there. *Here we are.* The blue haze no longer exists; the Rockies are only a part of the usual world, a juxtaposition of things, this stone shaped like a bench on the side of the road, this leafy canyon, this intense green, this gray, this normal light, those trout in the river. The Rockies are no longer the extravagant Erewhon, the Shangri-la my childish eyes had imagined. The blue haze has evaporated, fled, expanded to fill the sky.

From that day on I had to make a new start, reinvent the Rockies, learn how to see beauty in the flatness of ordinary reality. Fortunately, as the poet Edmond Jabès wrote, "the inside of stone is written." I watched, tried, learned, and made a few tentative steps toward the inside of things. But I never ceased to cherish the illusion, still longed to touch the blue haze hidden around the rock, to stroke the profile of the mountain.

The path toward the mountain of t'ai chi ch'uan is long and mysterious, its curves shrouded by the future. As one ascends, the landscape evolves, becomes vast and clear. Lights and colors, glimpses of the infinite, unexpected jolts. The distant grows near; the difficult becomes simple; what seemed easy turns out to be problematic. But the path winds on, and again, the obvious is turned upside down, the questions change.

As a rule, one starts on this adventure with naive certainty about its goal: becoming strong and handsome (or remaining so), learning self-defense, fighting old age, backaches, heavy legs. And no doubt a steady practice may largely fulfill these wishes. We will never know the total savings to the health care budget created by the assiduous practice of Asian disciplines such as t'ai chi ch'uan or yoga. It is a well-known fact that dancers are prone to osteoarthritis after the age of thirty-five, that tennis players suffer from tendinitis, soccer players from pulled muscles. Reaching the age of thirty, in most Western sports, marks the beginning of the end. An ex-champion *must* decline, renounce his art, gain weight, start a business....

The specific expectations created by the martial arts are given solidity by the advanced age of the masters. In all legendary tales about Chinese or Japanese masters there is at least one episode showing their serenity in the face of approaching death. In an art where the goal is not to dominate others but to surpass oneself, it seems logical there should be no end to progress. Progress merely changes its direction as the body changes. The aging master relies more and more on inner strength, which fosters ample compensation for the decline in muscular vigor. This progression toward the interior, by sparing muscles the hard work, helps to preserve the joints and strengthen the heart. All martial arts have an immediate effect on the cardiovascular system, on breathing, backaches, fevers, local aches and pains. But the benefit is more general: by dissolving blocked or sluggish circulation, by linking the different parts of the body, the practice improves one's mood and over-all well-being. Soon the attention given to the accuracy of one's gestures spreads into everyday life. More and more actions are performed consciously. And what a clever tool the body becomes when put to work this way! Solid legs, free arms, a more flexible chest....

At the same time, one develops an acute sensitivity to local discomforts: a stiff neck, an awkward posture, a headache. Without delay, consciousness sets out to find a solution, to work its way through the crowded block. Thoughts travel to the danger zone, helping to relax, stretch out, lighten the shoulders and neck. More often than not, such safety measures, taken early on, are sufficient to relieve the anxious tension. These therapeutic discoveries come to each of us, sooner or later, and confirm that we are growing on solid ground.

Meanwhile, the elusive goal moves away at each turn of the road, like the blue haze of the Rockies. Eclipsed by the fullness of the present experience, it hides in the future. Serious hikers know well that after a few hours of effort, they reach a paradoxical state in which the act of walking becomes the natural condition of the body, in which motion becomes a state. The aim ceases to be getting somewhere, to the warm refuge, a cup of hot chocolate. Motion is self-sufficient and the length of the path is part of its charm. During a long walk, the feet naturally find the stable position and the adequate rhythm in relation to the terrain; they direct the legs, which in turn swing the pelvis. The pendulum of the arms indicates the general pace. The regularity of the steps borders on immobility. The hiker has the impression he is floating, so solid his lower body feels, while his chest moves ever forward, following the invisible line drawn by the country-side, the continuous bass note of the path to follow, intensified yet unchanged by the rhythm of his arms and legs. Breathing unites the whole; the breath is to motion what rhythm is to music.

The instant becomes the heart of time. Once the hiker reaches this acute state, he opens up to the surroundings, takes it all in. "Look, this leaf has jagged edges; that rock, over there, looks loose.... These are small details one should notice while climbing. There is no point in hiking towards a faraway destination. It is on the sides of the mountains that life develops, not on the top. But of course, without the top there would be no slopes.... No hurry...."[8] The birds singing, the ever-changing light, the daisies, the squirrels, the rabbit holes, the clouds. The hiker's automatic pilot frees him of his body, of his gestures. He doesn't think about them any more. He is happy to keep on going. He doesn't try to solve the mystery of the mountain anymore. He gazes forward, that is enough. He goes forward.

Toward what destination?

Toward his second body, calmly pacing on the other side of the mirror: the twin body from the antipodes.

VII

Our gestures are the most intimate thing we have (we *are*). Rarely do we give them much thought; they accompany and carry us through life, too familiar to become conscious, silent witnesses of an invisible reality which, by its obscure presence, sustains our conviction that we exist.

Habit weaves a safety net, directions for use which allow us to navigate a thousand daily perils: to get dressed, wash, turn off the gas, empty the bathtub, lock the door, look both ways before crossing the street, walk down the subway stairs, smile to a familiar face. Among the innumerable gestures we perform every day, only a few are retained in the frail net of memory, usually those that escape habit: sidesteps, impulses, failures, first times.

Yet I will never forget J. P.'s emotion when, returning to his childhood home, he prepared to turn the handle of the French doors leading to the terrace. The bolt was stuck, just as it used to be twenty years earlier, and as he turned the handle he found himself avoiding a small protruding nail that had remained there all this time. Rediscovering the sensation of this familiar avoidance, repeated thousands of times, while pressing down the handle to open the door, he discovered the certainty, the private reality of his coming home. Memory of habitual gestures is a metaphor of the native land.

Meanwhile, life has flowed on, with its splendor, its ecstasies, its sorrows. Everything has changed:

countries, colors, words. The kingdom of childhood has lapsed into nostalgia, mourning for lost paradise, denials. And the nail still stood there as an unchanging witness, intact in the lock of the door. Yet the nail itself changes, in its own way, on a geological scale; the feeling of estrangement between a person and a nail comes from the tremendous difference in their time spans. Some day the French doors will fall to pieces and the nail will rust away in the ground. A hundred million years later, nothing will remain but a small red spot in a sandy desert. Should we care about the life expectancy of a nail?

We are unsettled by the strange time warp of animals' lives: a cat may live about nineteen or twenty years. How many times have my children worked out the "age" of our pets Maya, Dream, or Fifi by multiplying those years by seven? (Without doubt, this has been their greatest mathematical curiosity!) One might conclude that the shorter a lifespan is, the more intensely each moment should be experienced. Yet cats spend their days sleeping. (At night, though, they go on the rampage.)

In ordinary situations, we take for granted certain things: those peonies will last two or three more days, the cherry tree will bloom in the spring, this postcard will turn into dust long before that bronze statue does, when one of us dies the other will move to the country, and "the first one to fall asleep must wake up the other one in the morning." Time speaks to us in many voices, holds us tightly in its multiple webs. We move about within these endless shifts like fish in water, without giving them a thought.

The art of writing starts as a tool designed to prolong the life expectancy of thought, a means of communication between different points in time. A message sent from the past to the future, and vice versa, from the silent future to the turmoil of the past. We understand that the present is responsible for the past (perhaps even more than for the future), if in no other way than by filtering and endlessly rebuilding it with its own materials. The scholar Jean Bottero explains that the first Sumerian semi-pictographic writings are essentially aides-mémoire, kinds of lists meant as reminders of certain events—a shipment of oil, a change of dynasty—designed for those who have witnessed them. At this stage of the invention, only those who remembered an event could recognize the past in the signs representing it. It is only much later that the art of writing, refined, simplified, even alphabetized, becomes abstract enough to evoke the unknown, describe the foreign, depict the absent, the imaginary, the mind, the divine.[9] If fate is nothing else than a given situation in the weave of history, the art of writing is an attempt to transcend fate. It serves as a kind of mailbox between points in time, a counterweight to endurance.

Yet gestures shape time, thereby giving it permanence and volume. Writing about Auguste

Rodin,[10] Rainer Maria Rilke notes that during the Renaissance "great sculptural art uncovered the secret of human faces, and of the ever-growing human gesture." Rodin, says Rilke, tried to capture this immemorial gesture, flowing through the ages of the river of humankind, rushing towards the future; all this time, instead of aging, of fading, the gesture grows ever more vigorous. In this lies the power of Rodin's statues: "The dream ascends through his hands." Rilke watches Rodin holding his chisel, scraping, stroking, hammering, and sees the sculptor taking up where his predecessors stopped, his gestures are linked to those of Praxiteles and Michelangelo, and all together they—these billions of gestures!—form a long arabesque chiseled in the space-time of art. "This body could not be less beautiful than the antique ones, it had to be even more beautiful. Life had held it in its hands two thousand years more, working on it, hammering it day and night...."

In the same manner, words inside different books are connected by the long chain of human thoughts. Writing, for Rilke, is sculpting the inside of language. In this case, gestures don't matter much: anything can serve to write with, from the scribe's reed to my cherished computer. There is something romantic about the image of the scribe, and nostalgia for the fountain pen is touching, but I personally prefer the fast lane, the most efficient gesture, the most tractable. In writing, unlike sculpture, the gesture has no direct contact with the meaning. The abstract material of language cannot be touched. We may be moved by the sight of an autograph, but a poem is no better or worse for being scribbled with a ballpoint pen on a restaurant tablecloth or printed on Holland vellum. No matter how well you sharpen your pencil, no matter how soft your parchment, the meaning remains separated from its graphic representation by a gap, a jump, an interval. It must be this gap that the Chinese calligrapher attempts to fill, but in so doing he approximates the art of painting. Shitao: "Although painting and calligraphy define themselves as two distinct disciplines, their accomplishment is nevertheless of the same essence." Guillaume Apollinaire dreamed of himself as a calligrapher.

Rilke envies Rodin because he works directly into living matter. He imagines "beautiful, authentic fragments of language made ornate by their own mass." Proudly, he writes to the sculptor: "Now I know how to make men and women, children and old people." As if at the horizon of art there were a fixed point where one might touch the meaning of words, stroke beauty, seize the beating heart of the marble.

We know, we sense that in our universe every thing is connected. It is the old story of the butterfly's wing. From Colorado to the rue du Pré aux Clercs in Paris, a long chain of linked molecules strings its way across the ocean and its storms—the fragile flesh of fields, the asphalt, the concrete, the trees, Rodin's statues, my piano, the Indian subcontinent—all the nondescript objects thrown together at random which constitute the body of the world, in the midst of which we build our nests like careless kids. In this turmoil we search for rules, for symmetry, and we find them along with everything else; they even govern machines.

This labor of encounter and description has for sole support our quiet awareness of the material contiguity of things. There is nothing metaphysical about this statement; common sense defines matter by its property of forming a whole. This abstract knowledge has no effect on the pain of separation, but it does help restore the wholeness of one's being.

Into this material continuum, gesture brings shape, logic, limit: the signatures of life. "Feet can weep!" cries Rilke, contemplating *The Burghers of Calais,* sculpted one by one in the bronze of unspeakable pain.

It may well be that the unconscious is structured like language, but it also houses those silent inscriptions made in our psyche by gestures, those active deposits radiating day and night inside our bodies. Prolonged silence in no way stifles the voice of language, which never ceases to pursue its secret chatter. In the same way, prolonged immobility, unless one is in a deep coma, does not destroy motion, which is always there, latent, an embryonic presence in the living body. "It is possible that the study of gestures may lead us through a side door to dig up another, more archaic, form of the unconscious."[11]

Another kind of knowledge, parallel to language, is handed down from generation to generation through the meaningful chain of gestures, from a mother's embraces to the games of love. To achieve even a rough approximation of a *kata*[12] creates a link across the centuries with the bodies of the agile Shaolin monks who first codified it, resurrects their sensations, renews their experience. It creates a strange closeness with unknown people of another era, another place, so far away it seems it never existed. *(While making love, are we not immersed in our embrace as in an ancient reminder, linked by the long chain of molecules to prehistoric lovers?)*

Those monks really did exist, they ate and drank, tramped barefoot along dusty paths, and performed these very same motions in the open meadows. As this notion sinks in, we realize it is not a scene from a movie, but a new awareness that causes the same incredulous astonishment as when, through a telescope, Saturn's rings first appear in the summer sky. This is no photograph! The planet is there, unquestionably alive, in the same night, the same sky! The existence of the Shaolin monks in the distant past of the Middle Kingdom gives our awkward gestures a safe mooring, a symbolic support.

We are spellbound. Wonder arises at the exact point where thought meets the world. Yet motion is as foreign to language as apparent reality is to consciousness and as the monks of Shaolin are to the Latin Quarter. Like dreams, like Saturn's rings, the gesture defies words, frustrates description. Trying to cross the abyss with its fragile threads, writing risks everything, and grows more lovely for daring.

Who can describe a simple step? In 1886, Gilles de La Tourette, who lent his name to the tic syndrome (also known as Saint Vitus's dance), came up with a tentative hyperrealist description: "The left leg takes the weight as the right foot leaves the ground by rolling from the heel to the tips of the toes, which are the last to leave the ground; the entire leg is brought forward and the heel of the foot makes contact with the ground."[13] However accurate, there is no escaping the heaviness of this descriptive artillery. But let us not misjudge words. The fact that so many of them are needed to describe a simple step should not diminish their value; they have other things to do than to devise boring descriptions, and they are not as clumsy as they seem. It all depends on what makes them go.

Only the sign language used by the deaf, which is both efficient and light, can produce a faithful description of gestures, even if it does no more than copy them. (Sign language, which doesn't need syntax, enables the deaf to substitute for long sentences a few rapid gestures and to understand one another around the world.) What does our writing, deprived of pictograms, retain of the complex opacity of a stroke, of a dance step, of a finger pressing a piano key? Can one *write* this kiss?

He holds your face in his hands and his lips are everywhere at once, agile butterflies, feverish, urgent; wings fluttering around your lips, nostrils, eyelids, at the curl of your ear, on your forehead. Breezes, flights, clouds, leaves shaken by the wind, falling stars. Images rise and vanish in a whirlwind with the extreme softness (the exquisite pain) of these dreamy kisses: no sooner sketched than they evaporate, playing the high notes of motion's melody, the vanishing trail left by desire in its course across the body.

The kiss is erased the moment it appears, like the wave hitting the shore. Where does it go? *Where does the light go when I blow out the candle?* The gesture flies away, it can never be seized. Until the invention of the cinema, no gesture had ever survived itself except in paintings or photographs.

"Even the Mona Lisa, even Velasquez's *Méninas* can be interpreted not as static, eternal forms but as fragments of motion, as clips of a lost film.... As if, from the history of art, a silent call was raised to give freedom of movement back to the image."[14] By conferring motion to images, the cinema has transformed the memory of gestures, and to this day we are not yet fully aware of the consequences of this revolution. But in everyday life, erasure is still the very substance of each gesture, inscribing it on the tip of the past, as frail and meaningful as a fine coating of dust on a deserted temple.

VIII

A beautiful act is an island of absoluteness in an ocean of chance. The whole planet is enthralled by the Olympic Games because they embody this truth. The media may believe that they are exploiting our fascination for beauty, but in fact, they are serving it.

If we did not have this passion for the perfect motion, the Olympics would never happen; beauty is their secret goal, their undeclared fulcrum, their hidden foundation. The athletes may seem to be striving for the glory of the podium's top step; actually, they are struggling toward perfection, toward the absolute gesture, where the will of the gymnast and the rules of the game come together with the laws of nature. The record, the medal, the excitement of the media, are only added attractions compared to the joy of unity derived from the perfect gesture.

Remember the tiny Chinese gymnast at the 1992 Games who literally flew around her uneven parallel bars? She was like Noah's dove taking off from the deck of the Ark! Free, airy, unreal, this fifteen-year-old girl defied gravity with the ease of a bird skimming treetops. She looped, swung, circled, climbed through empty space. Her total mastery filled the set figures with grace, invention, magic. The air rustled around her. She could have gone no farther, no higher. The gold medal was merely confirmation.

The popularity of the Olympic Games is not due, as we naively believe, to our childish fascination for podiums, brilliant stages, and superstars. This belief underestimates our own wishes, our deepest yearning. The Games are indeed full of glitter and excitement and, yes, we are entranced by the *suspense* of the competition. But what we really love, what captures our soul, is the beauty of the skater's triple jump, the arc of the discus thrower's body. These are magic visions of freedom, on a par with Icarus' dream: they transcend nature's laws. The athlete submits to gravity in order to overcome it.

Shitao said, "complete domination of the Rule is the same as the absence of rules..., but whoever wishes to be without rules must first possess them." Eyes glued to the screen as we watch the Chinese gymnast, we realize that only a grueling apprenticeship has enabled her to attain such grace. And this ever-present knowledge merely adds to the pleasure of the performance. We admit with a certain jubilation—at least where others are concerned!—the idea that technical skill is the necessary prerequisite to ecstacy, the condition of freedom, the divine mother of athletes, dancers, practitioners of the martial arts, and pianists. This idea conforms to our beliefs: you can't get something for nothing, you have to suffer, etc. So it is only fair that technical skill is the queen of the Games.

When she performed, the gymnast's spirit became transparent, totally readable in every move she made. Suspended between sky and earth, the onlookers flew in unison with her gestures, attuned to her freedom, her confidence, as if they also could feel the smooth wooden bar in their hands. Her body's center of gravity, firmly rooted, seemed to serve as a moveable floor, giving her unshakable protection against falling. For the gymnast, as for the tightrope walker or the trapeze artist, an awkward movement is not an anecdote but a tragedy. Learning the craft consists of searching for the state of perfection where errors can no longer occur, become unthinkable.

Similarly, the pianist, working on a piece, aims at the level of excellence sufficient for the security which is to the soloist what the floor is to the dancer—an ability to go anywhere, like a mountain bike, ready to assume any risk. Control is the gateway to freedom. And freedom, of course, is the ultimate goal.

Many people are convinced that technical skill is distinct from interpretation, that a pianist works on his technique like a body-builder and subsequently adds "feelings" in order to construct, on this framework of virtuosity, the fine edifice of interpretation. In reality, technique is omni-present, even in the simplest passage. Amateur pianists tend to neglect the "easy" parts, where fingers run on like water from a fountain. Yet these unfixed passages may turn into weak points in a concert, when stage fright threatens. Without technical mastery, the performance remains cerebral, shaky; the amateur fingering a sonata imagines it more than he actually plays it. He does not *listen;* instead, he reads the score and dreams.

My friend D. claims that in very difficult pieces which call for rapid shifts along the keyboard, the sound obtained is in fact the opposite of the gesture producing it: the finger soars down, as if to prepare an explosion, but the sound is gentle. This misconception is the result of an optical illusion; the internal reality of a gesture is not always visible, but it necessarily coincides with the demands of the music—if there is music!

Both pianist and gymnast look up to technique as to a god confounded with the worship it arouses. In the execution of a t'ai chi ch'uan form, the visible mastery, the faithfulness to the outward form, are but one limited aspect, a first step acquired by imitation and repetition and which requires a specific use of memory, joining physical and mental concentration.

The real work only begins once the external form has been memorized, once the first level of the rule has been established. One then assumes that memory is reliable, that its job has been at least provisionally completed, and undertakes the long ascetic task of deepening, which leads toward an unending unveiling of the latent meanings in each gesture. (Just as in the Talmudic tradition, the commentary of the Biblical text, renewed with each generation, awakens new meanings which have been lying there dormant from time immemorial.) A modern master, performing a centuries-old Chinese kata, may rediscover forgotten teachings and ancient skills. But at an even deeper level, once a certain control has been achieved, each performance of a kata is a personal creation, however imperfect. We each have our own style.

To improve his technique, the student of t'ai chi ch'uan must dig ever deeper in search of the energy required by his gestures. Not only in his muscles but also in the internal organs—heart, lungs, stomach. And not only in these organs but also in the mysterious region of the belly which corresponds to no particular organ but to a feeling of warmth and strength: the tanden (also called the *hara*). Both imaginary and active, immaterial and concrete, the tanden is a sort of "pineal gland" where soul and body join. At a certain level, the reality of the tanden becomes an experienced and thus unquestionable truth. Above all, the martial arts teach a fine dialectic of skill and sensation: sensation points out the direction the technical search must take; in return, each technical progress brings forth new sensations.

Technical mastery is therefore not just a method but the very substance of the art, its condition of existence. Without reliable technique, good intentions lead to hell, delicate melodies turn syrupy, vital energy withers. To scorn technique is absurd and denies the very base, the very root. "Scorn of technique has its source in the hatred of beauty."[15]

If the archer's technique is perfect, his gesture will be accurate and the arrow will hit the bull's eye. The virtuoso, too, aims for the center, and there is no need to go and check the target: a beautiful sound proves the excellence of the motion which produced it. A beautiful gesture attests to its own efficiency; the value of the act and the mark it leaves upon the world are one and the same. As good old J. S. Bach used to say, "All you have to do is to push the key down at the right time."

What gives fullness to a chord? There are innumerable factors: the speed of your fingers, their angle, the curve of your wrists, the flexibility of your arms, the position of your body on the piano bench, your way of touching the keyboard, of leaning into it and springing back from it, the path your hands take from the previous notes, the accuracy of the pedal, your musical and visual memory, your knowledge of the score, your impetus, conviction, concentration. Without the unifying technique, as long as gaps remain in the puzzle, the performance remains unsteady.

How is one ever to master this random collection of rules, wishes, know-hows, and almosts? Technique is a jungle full of dangers, traps, heights, and faults. Two difficult bars in a Bach fugue, an indomitable page by Chopin ... and the millstone rolls back down the hill. Technique is a monster, a hydra: no sooner does one sever its heads than they grow back. Pianists hate technique but prostrate themselves at her feet, they weave crowns for her, trembling at the idea that they might lose the favors of this Fury who signals their failures.

At times we sets out to tame her too fast, and she rears up, tears off with the bit in her teeth and jumps over the sound barrier in a mad cavalcade, leaving us breathless, worthless. Attacked head on, technique feigns surrender; for a few hours, the pianist hopes the difficulty is vanquished. But the next day, the fingers slip again, nothing is left, almost nothing.... Climb up the hill again!

How to escape discouragement?

Obviously this isn't the issue. What I want to know is, how could you ever wish to escape such a delightful captivity?

IX

What happens to William Tell at that crucial instant when, surrounded by the possibility of failure, he aims at the apple on his son's head? "If Tell's hand had shaken...." In his book on Liszt, Vladimir Jankelevitch compares the hero adjusting his crossbow to the virtuoso scaling the arpeggios of an *étude d'exécution transcendante* toward the heights of an F-sharp. The archer and the pianist take the same crazy risks. Tell's dilemma is clear: "Save his son and country or condemn both of them in one movement of the finger; is it possible to experience greater stress? Life and death depend on the shot of an arrow; how narrow the margin between Charybdis and Scylla, between infanticide and servitude, between what is still possible, and what is too late. Everything is hanging by a thread, everything depends on the diameter of the apple! However, as a rule, an arrow released by a skilled archer's bow *must* hit the center."[16] And we exclaim: "How lucky!"—senselessly reducing a masterpiece to a vulgar miracle.

Of course, the fear of missing an F-sharp shouldn't be as tragic as the terror of killing your own child; in comparison, it may even seem ridiculous. What is at stake, at the worst? The virtuoso's career, reputation, self-respect. Raw eggs and overripe tomatoes. Shame, fear, and guilt pertain only to his inner state, his subjective being. The world has not been shattered and even the listeners' ears (provided they even noticed the error) have suffered only passing discomfort. For William Tell it's another story altogether; the dangers he faces are terribly, intensely real. At stake is the fate of Switzerland, the life of his child. The hero holds History in his bent fingers.

However, their ambition is the same: both archer and pianist must face the absolute nature of what their art demands. Any imperfect, blurred, or awkward gesture is disqualified from the start. "Perfect aim" becomes an imperative, a vital necessity, a tightrope walk. Yet in the West, perfection can never be permanent; it is only a special moment, the climax of a tragedy, an apogee. In the East, perfection means much more. It is a constant quest, a reason to live and to die. "The aim is not to attain an instant of illumination but to create a lasting state in oneself."[17]

"The idea of virtual danger, of death at one's heels, is an intrinsic part of the soloist's solitude," writes Jankelevitch. The pianist undergoes a trial by fire, "an anxiety known as stage fright."[18] Stage fright zeroes in diabolically on the sensitive area and immediately strikes the relevant part of the body, causing the pianist's fingers to tremble, the singer's vocal cords to fail, the actor's memory to lapse. Being a side effect of the inflated ego, it easily locates the vulnerable spot. True art does not suppress stage fright but ignores it—or, better still, converts it into additional energy. Drawn deep from the other side of talent, it enhances the performance.

The only way to attain the mental state enabling one to overcome danger is to forget oneself, to dismiss the ego, to let the ultimate goal (music, the life of a child) fill up the whole inner space. Then, they say, the musician melts into the music, the archer becomes the target. "He does not aim to pursue an exterior goal with a bow and arrow, but to fulfill something inside himself." Can you picture a Zen master paralyzed with stage fright?

The entire perspective is reversed; self-forgetfulness, being the essential means to concentration, the only road to perfection (pianistic, martial ...), ceases to be a tool in order to become the very object of the quest. The result of the gesture thus surrenders to its aim. Here lies the secret motivation underlying the pianist's or the t'ai chi practitioner's inhuman perseverance: a certain desired state of consciousness. Music would then merely lead the way toward another state of being. In the same way, combat in a martial art would ultimately serve to reveal his real inner state to the combatant himself.

"The shot does not have the required ease unless it surprises the archer himself." The surprise is in proportion to the revelation. Where, then, is William Tell standing, if not in the quiet confidence of the Zen master who shoots blindfolded, seventy-five feet from the target? "Something shoots," says Herrigel's master. The risk of error is reduced to zero because "the archer is also aiming at himself." If he reaches the point of total lucidity, the arrow will fly off of its own accord and hit the center. *(Once locked in there it could vibrate forever!)* External victory merely serves to confirm the correct aim of the soul.

Need it be said that this particular state of flawless unity between thought and motion is made possible only through mastery of technique? It isn't the usual everyday consciousness which enables the pianist to unravel garlands in Chopin's *23rd Étude,* but an extreme lucidity built on the gradual acquisition of well-tempered automatisms, and a deep knowledge of the musical text which surfaces only at the right moment and immediately retreats into the storerooms of memory. The depth of these well-known gestures is the foundation on which confidence and freedom are built. True interpretation requires a saturated memory. To exit time, we have to pass through it.

The exact moment at which the archer releases his arrow is removed from ordinary time. It belongs to another dimension, a sort of incorruptible actuality. "Art is devoid of art, a shot is no longer a shot, the teacher becomes a student, the master becomes a novice, and the beginning becomes the culmination," says Herrigel. From this point of view, that time can be abolished is no longer a question but an experience. Tell's arrow darts into this parallel world—and arrives before leaving the bow. "Do not win after you have struck; strike after you have won," says the master swordsman Miyamoto Musashi.[19] This only appears to be a paradox; in the master's gesture, art without art cancels time and, therefore, chance as well. The gesture precedes itself. The French painter Ernest Dégas also found this to be so, comparing brush techniques to the beauty of the dance: "Nothing in art should be left to chance, not even movement." Every shot by Herrigel's master is identical to every other, super-imposed in the absolute present of certainty. No chance is left, no unknown possibility, no past, no future.

In Kurosawa's film *The Seven Samurai*, during the encounter between the young hero and the old swordsman, there is one crucial instant just as the fight is about to begin. The hero already knows he has lost, and surrenders to his master. Yet neither one of them has moved. At this level of consciousness, the fight is no longer necessary. Martial art becomes the guarantor of peace. And as we all know, music has charms to soothe the savage beast.

X

We're no longer thinking about it. We're there. Here.

The wooden floor offers its soft geometry.
The golden wood and the venetian blinds seem
to soak up sounds, muffling the cries and screeches
of the city. The silence is inhabited by overlapping
noises: the ticking of the wall clock, the dog in
the courtyard.

The pain in my thighs has reached a residual
state and no longer bothers me. Good news. You
can tame pain, make it dissolve in the ringing
bells of Saint Thomas d'Aquin. It can even become
tolerable without losing intensity. Behind me,
someone stretches. I want to turn around to find
out which one of us has failed. I resist temptation
and chalk up another point against the enemy.
In the distance Paris rumbles, gray in the light
rain, full of people dashing for cabs. I like the
voice of my city, its gentle murmur, its background
noise, its perpetual exchange of secrets, its endless
cacophony. I like, above all, to hear it from a
distance, from a quiet place. It is so quiet here!

Once relieved from the specter of pain,
accuracy of the posture becomes the new goal:
expand the contraction in the legs, try a slow
rocking motion, forward and backward, pressing
against the floor as if to leave a footprint, as if to
play the piano with the toes.... Fingers and toes,
their spirit is the same, elastic and powerful. The
surrounding noises have been stilled; the silence
they harbored appears at last in the glory of the
white morning.

At the heart of the movement hides the truth of the fleeting instant. In the West, the fleeting, the transient, are only excuses for nostalgia, gone before they have had time to exist, immediately stored away in memory, stuck in the instantaneous transmutation of the past into the future. It seems to us, wrongly, that the flight of time disqualifies reality.

But the instant is time's punctuation, a flood of eternity into the flux of time. A moment not listed in any dictionary or database. Neither the sun stopped in its orbit, nor the Red Sea opening up, nor Vinteuil's *"petite phrase"* in Proust's *A la Recherche du Temps perdu* are listed in the catalog of great monuments. The instant tears time up and floods it with the infinite. Rilke spoke of these "moments of high intensity where eternity seems to flow from on high to fill the day."[20]

Such moments come in many assorted colors. *Leaves shaken by the wind. Delightful presence, presence. At the tip of the fingers, the fervent swell of the skin. A mosaic of surfaces drawn to the center. Whirlwinds. Maelstroms. Throbbing. Feverish planning in the forge of legends.* In music, the indefinite pause suspends the tempo. Music, the art of numbers, perfects its shape by slightly transgressing the law of proportions that structures it, as exuberant foliage develops around the unrelenting axis of rhythm. The emotion born from sound produces its own temporality, as if musical time were not relative but rooted in itself. When

Horowitz plays Schubert, time veers off,
cancelled by a pianissimo; it fades away and rolls
up like the stormy sky in Isaiah's prophecy.

The message of our dreams nightly confirms
the treachery of clocks. I grew aware of their
shameful lie as a teenager, thanks to an early film
by Robert Enrico, *Incident at Owl Creek Bridge,*
a black-and-white feature lasting about twenty
minutes. Adapted from a short story by Ambrose
Bierce, it takes place in the South during the Civil
War. The screening of this little-known masterpiece was a personal revelation; to this day its
echoes reach me through the mists of the past.

Surrounded by soldiers in a gray and white
landscape, a Confederate prisoner in shirtsleeves
is walking to the place of execution, a scaffold
erected in the middle of a wooden bridge. From
the very start you like this man who wants to live,
you want to save him. But the executioner is
placing the noose around his neck. Facing the
river, he is standing on a board over the water.
All the soldier will have to do is yank the board
from under his feet. Drums are beating. The sky
is getting darker. The river roars below.

Suddenly the board is pulled back, the rope
tightens like the cord of a bow, but while the
soldiers are shooting furiously a miraculous
bullet slices the rope, and the prisoner falls into
the river with the rope still round his neck.
Dodging bullets, he swims away. He is lucky, he

evades the shooting soldiers. He swims for a long time, then lands breathless on a little beach at the foot of a lawn. In the distance is a grand colonial mansion, with an elegant perron and veranda. A woman in a white dress runs towards him, her arms spread wide. He is home. Alas, his joy is too great. He runs towards the woman in the white dress, but his footsteps drag him backward, toward the soldiers in pursuit. She is there, though, waiting for him, greeting him. Oh! If only he could cross the lawn! But he keeps slipping back, as if sucked in by the void. This wavering image opens our eyes at last: we are back where we started. On the scaffold, the prisoner's body hangs lifeless, head forward, feet dangling.

"Soleil, cou coupé."[21]

The rope did not break. Time itself shattered like a crystal, trembling under the insistent caress of hope. Divested of all its temporal finery, the soul stands naked. Along with the prisoner in a white shirt we have, in the space of a film, experienced the expansion of time caused by the rush of desire. A mad burst of thoughts proves capable of absorbing reality into timelessness, like an emergency exit. A mad explosion of life, a passing redemption, open arms, a white dress, a soft lawn. Humankind's capacity to transcend, through its visions, the imminence of death is at the source of every creative act, however small and hidden.

A tenth of a second, the duration of a sigh ... such moments should be celebrated. This highly subjective, immeasurable, rebellious time should be taken seriously, deciphered, fully experienced. It should be examined, in fact, as a fragment of reality can be examined, a piece of golden dust, a little yellow patch on a wall in Delft from a Vermeer painting. What relationship is there between the atmosphere of a Parisian street this September morning—the wind is cool, most people still have tanned skin and relaxed manners, shop windows are being redone—*and the daily news?* Shouldn't "history" also relate these brush-strokes, these cross-capers, these giggles, these timeless intervals between time? Who is to say where the event begins, where the anecdote ends?

Crumbs of reality, bursts of light, these tiny experiences appear as parts of reality, of light, of silence, just as Cézanne's brushstrokes are part of the mountain. In order to take them into account, to "understand" them, it would be enough to acknowledge their unquestionable status as particular experiences. And to give this particular intimacy the essential place it should have in the narration of a truly *human* history, enlarged, improved, lit from within, enriched by its own shadows. "The meaning of History is not revealed by the process of its evolution but by the disruptions in its apparent continuity, in the flaws and accidents, where the sudden arrival of the unexpected interrupts the flow, revealing in a flash a fragment of original truth." [22]

With the two sides of its nature in agreement, history would be like a torn cloth rewoven, a tree reunited with its roots. The breaks would cease to be fantasies or hallucinations and take on meaning, become signs. Silence could at last deliver its untimely message, showing the way to reality. Were Dostoevsky's epileptic fits medical or metaphysical? Who cares? Only the change in consciousness is real for him at the time it happens. Epilepsy doesn't forbid revelation. And the words of the poet do not coincide at any point with the monotone of the telephone time service.

Belonging of necessity and "simultaneously" to these radically estranged temporalities is one of the great chasms in the human condition. Depending on the civilization, reality tends either toward the license of dreams or the regularity of clocks. Since Babylon, clocks have made great progress: chronology reigns as master of our history books, which claim to present only "facts." But what really happened in the secret wells of conscience during those long centuries filled with massacres, epidemics, and despotisms? This is Wim Wenders' question, in his film *Wings of Desire*, about the people in the street today, but it could be enlarged to the streets of the past: what were they thinking about, the busy people in this Parisian street one autumn morning in 1775? Was the wind chilly? How fast did the children run on their way to school? Was it even the same street? What do two sunrises separated by centuries have in common?

Walter Benjamin wanted to "save the past" by listening to history's silences, in which the voices of the vanquished can be heard. Could this method be applied to one's personal life? Think of all the lost moments of an ordinary day which might deserve to be "rescued"—an attic full of miniature events (bus stops, waiting rooms) which, properly dusted off, may unveil endless poetic treasures. Such is Benjamin's political program: read history inside out. "Release what is radically new from each moment of the past."[23] Release the perfume of the evening air as it is felt in the fields of Combray. Who could object to such a project?

Will we be brave enough, in the near future, to replace clock time with a "qualitative time where every moment is lived for its incomparable singularity"? If inner time replaces measured time, if every instant is a unique angel raised skyward, then the ordinary historian is useless. Only the artist can write history as it should be written, inside out, from the other side of the present time. *An Incident at Owl Creek* does not take place during the screening, but between the white shirt and the shadow of the rope, between the eye and the ear, the hope and the fear, the soldiers' bullets. In the margins.

The black holes of our psyche, saturated with condensed time, house the interior studio where our personal scenarios are made to fit our acts. Free flight: the wind is rising, the soldier shoots, the rope breaks; trying to survive, the prisoner's soul springs toward the river and we grip the arm-rests of our seats to refrain from doing a feverish breaststroke in our seat. A story is being told, filled with our dreams. Escape. Survival. Swimming. Bullets whistling. Freedom. White dress. Open arms.

The reality of this illusion is fascinating. A story is put together, structured like a suspense film, in a fraction of a second suspending time in a dying man's consciousness. The death of the Confederate soldier is no more real than the frantic interlude of his escape. Anyway, according to the rules of good storytelling, death is not a conclusion. The end of the film is nothing else than the limit of the dream. The instant contains eternity as a tear contains the ocean.

And where were you, last night, in that car driving across the Seine? And your thoughts? Did they linger with your gaze on the brilliant dome of the Grand Palais floating like a spaceship among the chestnut trees? Who is telling the hidden story? Shakespeare, Hugo, Rilke, Proust, Musil, Zweig, Ophüls? Each of us elects his own heroes. The breaststroke of a dying rebel also has its beauty.

XI

In t'ai chi ch'uan, the breaststroke crosses the air. Motion rocks on its own waters. The image of the swimmer slowed down by the liquid mass, as we move about in thin air, conveys to our bodies the dreamy majesty of transatlantic ships. Space thickens as our movements slow; it becomes water, honey, dough, glue.

Keeping the whole body afloat in this elastic element requires constant care. Release your consciousness for a wink and the air thins, becomes light and easy to bridge; lack of attention leads to stiffness, stagnation, stops and starts. At the lowest level of awareness, these breaks in tempo appear as voids, blanks, dead angles. (Simply noticing them implies that one is again paying attention. After all, attention is what discipline asks for, the way one would ring for the maid.) Consciousness also records its failures in our gestures.

Just try missing that step on the way down into sleep. There comes the blank. Falling asleep, I feel fine, *I'm on my way*, and then the earth vanishes from under my feet although I haven't left my bed. I dream without dreaming that I fall without falling. It is an instant fall, and stops at once. I feel as though I have moved into another world, parallel yet contiguous and identical to the previous one. My entire body is shaken by this jerk, as if by an electric shock. It could be easily shown on a screen. The gesture of an arm, interrupted by a few black inches, giving the impression of a jump, a break.

The jolt has thrown me into another world, like an instant change of skin. It has taken me across an abyss. The electric leap holds me back a few more seconds, on the edge of sleep, at the border. Dreams take their time getting ready beneath the eyelids, the fresh sheets and evening's idle thoughts, waiting for the great departure towards oneself.

Transitions, intervals. A three-masted ship sets sail for Africa, ruffling its majestic wings in the twilight gold of a Hanseatic port. The voyagers, tiny commas curled toward the land, blink in the brutal rays of the sun, soon to be humbled by the night. A bird has made its nest high up in the rigging. A siren blows, Poseidon's horn. It resonates against the city walls and mingles its echoes with the fleeting light. Traces of the future permeate the painted present. Only the sunset will allow darkness to enter, discreetly. The sphere known as earth travels deeper into the shapeless, blinking night.

Light has never been purer than tonight, while a painting by Claude Lorrain burns my eyelids. I do not know if I am awake or asleep. Is it a dream, this golden light pouring out before my spellbound eyes? Are they open or closed? Am I in the living room, with a book on my knees? Am I writing these words? Am I asleep? It hardly matters. I'm here, I'll stay. It feels good to be in this luminous country, bathed in the shifting light kindled by the fury of stars. How marvelous is this motionless time. Look, the ship is still there, under full sail beneath my eyelids, heeling gently to the breeze, proudly present, as repetitive as a spark perpetually alight, like those silly birthday candles that reignite after they're blown out.

The foghorn booms three times. The bearded god is calling; the curtain rises on the ocean spreading its blue skirt around the earth, sketching the continents. The voyagers' faces seem worried yet elated. The tender light of the port grows pale above the endless expanse of the waters, beneath a turbulent gray sky tinged with gold. The adventure is forever beginning again. The voyagers wave their handkerchiefs. Time grows denser.

Convinced of their own lucidity, scientists bring about atomic fission. Believing himself to be awake, the dreamer revels in the fission of time. Dreams claim to be real. The dreamer rarely knows he is dreaming and the minute he does, he prepares to wake up or to change dreams. The reverse does not hold true: reality does not pretend to be a dream. Or maybe it does. . . . But where were we?

In broad daylight, as in dreams, small shocks still occur. Slips of the tongue, tics, awkward moves or thoughts, things dropping and breaking. We politely put up with them, hoping to forget about them. Their obscure power has been haunting us for such a long time! We are used to compromising with our follies, to carelessly pushing aside our weird thoughts. Negligently, we build frail passages above the faults in our consciousness, hoping to forget them, as if we had no other choice.

This makes the job of keeping up the required continuity a most exacting task for us, poor wretches bent beneath the rod, absentminded, scatterbrained, hurried creatures that we are, with our crazy minds and our flickering attention. It takes months, years of practice to oil the transitions, to eliminate the hesitations, the jerks and jolts. The dream of the perfect kata looms on the horizon, where continuity from one move to the next and from mind to body promises to be unbroken. Where the sequence of our movements becomes a single sentence, a unique gesture, a continuous bass note.

For years, my daughter Judith relentlessly asked: "Where does the sky begin? How high up? Above the houses?"

"The sky begins on your tummy, around your fingers, at the tip of your nose, above your bed when you sleep. When it rains, it makes a halo. The wings are for free."

"But, Mom, where does it start, for real?"

"Around your hair, in front your eyes ... goes through you when you breathe...."

"You mean the real sky, the one floating up on the roof, it comes down this far?"

Unbelieving, she studies her hands, her feet, her scraped knees, looking for the sky floating over the roof (so blue, so calm).

The martial arts prove the existence of air. Likewise, at the end of his life, Velasquez no longer painted objects but the space between them. The combatants' bodies are not separated by a void but joined together by the very substance of the atmosphere, by their neighboring breaths. The truth of their movements, their efficiency, depends on their subtle perception of this invisible link. However, motion seems to have no effect on the volatile element. No more than water does air retain memory. It is usually defined by its very passivity, except for strong winds or ocean breezes. Like time, it is tractable and remains untouched while being penetrated.

Air is not the same as space, but to *feel* this, one first has to *imagine* it. Here is the paradox: seeing precedes vision, the sensation precedes the thought that makes it happen. At the very instant he shoots, the archer experiences from within the passage of the air around the arrow in a kind of simultaneous echo. And when the pianist's finger-tips touch the cool ivory keys, the resistance of the hammers, the vibration of the strings, all related to the composer's long vanished thoughts, the initial contact with the instrument spreads at once through hands and wrists into the deepest corners of his being. The contiguity of things can be overwhelming.

The thickness of air is but one of the classic mental images used by teachers from the East to increase the compactness of motion. Any image will do, as long as its evocative power wraps the entire body in a tight weave, eliminating the frequent jolts of ordinary life. From the spine to the toes and the facial expressions, sensations and gestures become conscious enough to submit to technique.

Mind you, this active body is not viewed anatomically; its organs, like everything else in the world, are mere figments upon which the mind works. The body might become, for example, an immense bag of skin in which liquid circulates freely. Miyamoto Musashi says: "You must learn, through the nature of water, the nature of the spirit. Be it a drop or an ocean, water adopts the shape of its container, be it square or round."[24]

Kenji Tokitsu comments on this aquatic metaphor: "It is an analogy between the body and a flexible container filled with liquid. Methods of attack can be derived from this analogy; strength is thought of as the shifting of liquid inside an elastic bag of skin. The impact of blows changes totally with the idea that they ripple throughout the body like waves in a liquid mass. If you view your opponent's body as a rigid statue, you will think of attacking him with the equivalent of a hammer, and in order to perfect your technique of attack you will try to harden your fists. On the contrary, what is important is not to hit something hard but to initiate a tremor which will disturb the liquid."[25]

The mental image is the impulse opening the way to technical skill. More than a simple metaphor, it is a possible interpretation of reality. In order to give consistency to my touch on the keyboard, my teacher Boucourechliev presses on my forearm. ("Resist me! Don't crumble like that!") And, as if by magic, my fingers feel like they are sinking into the keys, which have become elastic. The image can, at times, be vivid enough to replace reality. I try to sink my feet into the floor of the dojo as into muddy ground—and it gives, like a trampoline.

These are performative metaphors (a speech is considered performative when its wording constitutes an act in itself, as when the king announces, "I abdicate!"—saying so equals doing it). Once you've experienced this, all you need to do is think about it. The effect of these metaphors is irresistible, almost automatic; the intensity of the image leads to a natural correction of the posture, to a change in the position of the forearm protecting the face.

At the beginning, the use of these images may cause anxiety, because of their magical effect. Can an imagined vision change the real world? Is this auto-suggestion logical, is it reasonable? Is it not another version of the infantile belief in the power of wishful thinking? However, the practical efficiency of these enigmatic images is above question; it is in proportion to the mind's control over motion. Uproot a tree, plant a tree, walk in the mud, glue your hands to the distant wall, pull a string from the roof to the top of your head, push and pull at the same time, move without moving. Give birth to contradictory tensions in every part of your body. Such are the tricks. A metaphor can change the twist of a muscle, and from there, in stages, alter the situation of the entire body. *Here we are again.*

"I say: air is the ghost of the world!"

My tiny daughter Judith shouts aloud so that I can hear what she is saying through the banging and rattling of the old open car. Her long blonde hair swings out of the window, her cheeks are pink with delight. Beneath the 2 hp Citroën's canvas roof, as we drive along the beach, it takes only a slight leaning out to capture the full strength of the wind on our faces, arriving from Africa to our beloved island, laden with the scent of sea and wildlife. The bumpy, uneven road changes our coach into a popcorn popper.

"I say: air is the ghost of the world!"

Air fills the space between living beings the way blanks connect these written words, the way oceans join the continents of the world. In Asian disciplines such as yoga or t'ai chi ch'uan, the experience of breathing adds reality to the invisible, gives faith in space, in the existence of air.

In Japanese *Budo* as in the Hebrew Bible, breath is but the visible aspect of the spirit (the same word in Hebrew, *ruah*, means breath and spirit[26]). Pervaded by breath, the body is filled with consciousness. If it is immutably centered, it connects to the world through all its pores and portholes; liberated from fineries, exaggerations, fakes, its movements are adequately garbed; enlivened by the spirit, by the ruah, like Shitao's paintbrush: "When the mind forms a clear vision, the brush goes to the root of things."

Curves are unmistakable. A t'ai chi ch'uan kata, performed by a master, possesses the sovereign grace of a Matisse in motion. (Although in his paintings, motion is born in no time.) Economy of means, purity of the line, precision of rhythm, accurate breathing, power.... Strangely, only total surrender to reality opens the way through the clouds of appearance to the light of the pure line, the clear vision, the unique brushstroke, the perfect melody.

It is not just on a canvas that respecting the laws of the prism enables one to capture the life inside the colors. T'ai chi ch'uan uses gravity to create harmony. It records the heartbeat of our inner voice, attuned to the power of the universe. It proves nothing; it *teaches* opening. Between the inside and the outside, between experience and appearance, it builds a bridge, opens an inter-section, lights a lamp.

The gesture may be defined by its result, but its existence derives from the inner feeling which makes it grow. Only sensation makes motion real.

XII

Dizzy with white wine, we stand and wait for our coats. The restaurant is about to close. The waiter is wiping the table. A lock of gray hair fallen over his eyes makes him look grumpy. In your eyes, I read the tenderness of despair. On the other side of the glass doors, the Parisian street swallows its passers-by. Faces seem to turn on and off in the blue and green flashing neon lights. You can't see what they think, not any more than you can see the motion of the clock's hands. It is time to leave, to hurry off into the darkness.

Hand in hand we weave our way along the dragon's arteries, following the signs. We walk fast, as if followed. It is nighttime, but the color red dominates wherever there is light: bars, cafés, Chinese restaurants. Red lights are precious gems on the skin of the urban beauty. Late at night, under the trees, down on the quays of the Seine, one can hear the wooden barges slowly rotting in the moonlight.

In the pedestrian zone, sheltered just enough from the insult of traffic, we are surprised by our footsteps echoing in the heart of the town. Listening to oneself walking in a deserted street is a rare pleasure, as rare and wonderful as being fully aware of one's breathing. The difference in our steps melts into a syncopated harmony. The pounding of our soles defines the contours of the street and populates the air.

A light soprano sends sputtering trills down at our feet; the sound comes from an old radio on a balcony, behind a pile of rusty metal, next to a bare tree. From the balcony, a little girl tosses a ball of chewed bubble-gum which bounces off a glass roof and lands in a puddle. We laugh. Your hand presses mine gently, as if holding a bird lightly so as not to hurt it. I feel my pulse begin to throb. Far away, on the boulevard, the traffic's pulse slows down for the night. I like the pale blue of your shirt at the fold in your neck. Now the radio switches to the shanai *of an Indian raga: ribbons of moonlight dance on a mountain lake. Venice offers its awed visitors such mobile ecstasies, enhanced by the rotting smell of the lagoon.*

She has agreed to explore Paris, of course. She's in love, the idiot. They wander north and south under bridges and along arcades, and stand in bars. Life is good while he's here, holding her hand like a bird. The word "warm" *does not begin to cover the wild rush flowing inside her from her toes to her hair, and farther. She instantly files this moment away in her secret archives. Her faith is so naive!*

She decides to remember it all, every minute detail. This fragment of space-time will become a treasure. The drunkard snorting at them as he passes by, a plastic hanger in his hand, musicians playing jazz near the café, flooded in the bright yellow light from the parasols, her lover's profile, his thoughtful eyes, his gaiety, the ruffling of her skirt against her thighs, the youth of the summer, the tenderness of Paris.

She has not yet learned that memory doesn't take orders but goes its own way, like a cat. The moments one wishes to recall are the first forgotten. It's only

natural—they are so heavy, so full of secret
thoughts. They sink at once like overladen barges.
She will remember this love, that's for sure, and
maybe this exalting vision of the city, but what will
remain of the beer they drank at the counter of the
Buci café, listening to a group of excited students?
Life is so long, and hope so stubborn.

She weighs her steps as she chooses her words,
one by one, calmly; she slows her breathing, looks
into the narrow streets, at peoples' faces, at yellow
lights, at arcades. Later, when it is all over, she will
be able to tell this story.

Settled at the entrance to the métro, *an old tramp*
sneers as they go by, ironic, vaguely envious, nailed
to the ground by fatigue. The tramp occupies my
thoughts for a moment. One would like to believe
that laziness and drunkenness have a special
meaning, that they aren't just factory defects. What
if they were the flip side of a torn ideal? To fall so
low, they must have come from very high, so high
that they could not help but feel ashamed about the
way the world goes round. Is the tramp's apathy a
secondary effect of his rejection of social reality?

There is no good reason why incurable distaste for
society should produce the fetid type of the Western
drunkard, while in India those who renounce
society are deeply honored. They are not stepped
on, trashed in jails or madhouses, forced to take
showers. The Indian sannyasin *are not tramps but*
objects of worship among the Hindus, because they

have chosen solitude and begging. They are given flowers and food. Their painted faces, lofty smiles, extravagant hairdos, bare feet, everything about them expresses harmony. Which system is telling the truth? The one that honors and cares for its philosophers, its rebels? Or the one that pushes them into the gutter?

These thoughts warmed me up as our steps led us near the edge of the night. From outside, one might have thought we were tensed toward a goal. But we had none, save to make this night a lasting one and to savor its taste. Our whims took us from Montmartre to the Pont des Arts and to the yellow parasols of Buci. From time to time, postmodern Bateaux-mouches daubed their lunar paintbrushes over the facades. Defenseless in these unreal lightings, the riverbanks became spectral. Beneath the chestnut trees of Ile Saint Louis, the Seine parted her legs and the smell of the river was overwhelmed by the nostalgic scent of the leaves.

My love wrapped the night in a magic cloak. In this splendid decor I decided, with the ridiculous fervor of the young, to store away in my living memory a single image, a single impression: this weight, this warmth around my curled hand. Can't stupid little souls hurt by love be repaired? They fix breasts and smooth wrinkles, don't they?

XIII

Have moments of wonder become unthinkable
in our sick history, reduced to glimpses of stolen
joy, hidden behind the monotony of days? An ice
cream at intermission, a daisy in a poem, a stolen
kiss, an oboe solo in a Bach cantata, a grove of beech
trees at the height of autumn—are they merely
vanishing points, stage whispers, emergency exits?

We have the feeling that eternity, our Eurydice,
has veiled her light. Her wing of mystery brushes
past us at times, but she flits away as soon as we
try to tame her. She grows wan in our museums,
suffocates in our clocks, and as she lays dying her
weakened strength radiates watery rays devoid of
warmth. The clamor of hydraulic drills, interest
rates, political maneuvers and the like thrusts
her into remote corners on the edge of silence.
Seemingly ashamed of itself, history seeks to expel
its dregs but only vomits its soul.

Far from here, in the secret of Asia's
mushrooming cities, placid eternity can still be
encountered at the four corners of time, through
the tiny things that survive modern industry: a
gesture, a greeting, a poem, a bouquet, a brushstroke. It is the great blossoming of "almosts" in
the cathedral of the absolute. These fully aware,
concentrated gestures, are they prayers? They
must at least be signs; they contain a decipherable
meaning and refer to an ideal. From the point of
view of beauty, all these gestures are the same
provided they are accurate; they light up at dusk,
like the stars.

Another eternity, another escape out of historical time is offered by Hebrew ritual.[27] Even if it gets entangled in the tormented branches of the human adventure, the time of myths is immutable, like a magic scarf which cannot be torn. Thus an event which, for mysterious reasons, rises to the level of myth—for instance, the Exodus from Egypt—remains, for observant Jews, more "real" than last week's pogrom. Not because it has actually happened, but because it endures and occurs again every year during the holy days. The never-ending return of the calendar actualizes memory. The event never ceases happening. Attracted by the present time, the Biblical past unfolds in the waking dream of study and the meditation of the ritual.

This reality from elsewhere, tucked away in consciousness, makes life bearable. If the struggle against Pharoah is more real than what happens to me today, a redeeming distance is established between the historical experience and the pain it causes. Thus the Biblical text becomes a source of permanent narrative solace, as if ancestral history were taking place on this very day, beneath the apparent history of our time. As if it pertained more to the present day than the much-too-real history of the Jews in this century.

It is not yet Doomsday, but something is coming to an end, one can feel it. There are no beaches beneath the pavement, only parking lots, and the future is no longer radiant. Sliding back into childhood, our culture puts up a show to please itself. The cult of quantity neglects "Quality" or spreads it over the surface of unshapely objects "like tinsel on a Christmas tree."[28]

Television displays its compulsory ballet of shadows. After the Ages of Bronze, of Iron, of Writing, of Coal, of Plastic, here come Virus and Hologram, AIDS, the Bronx, senior citizens' homes, traffic jams at rush hour, the ugly Tour Montparnasse. (Even strawberries have lost their flavor!) And the make-believe of the media: crumbling welfare, cadmium oysters, poisonous transfusions, starving kids, Sarajevo, Somalia, neo-Nazis. Our Western world seems to be blocked in the uterus of a sterile era, in the ruined decor of a breathless tragedy, a world "deprived of atmosphere."[29]

History annihilates its dreams by fulfilling its fantasies, and buries its tales under the filth of its crimes. As a blank check granted to horror, the shadow of the Sho'ah heartens the perpetration of modern massacres. The "malaise" diagnosed by Freud, with its steadily worsening symptoms, is not merely a consequence of our civilization, a perverse side effect of its shortcomings, but its very source, its manure. Everyone knows that waste fertilizes weeds. Our wretched heap of secrets fertilize our actions, our products, our creations, bestowing on them the blunt, flashy aspect of modernity. Their smell betrays them: the stink of hot plastic in the Parisian subway, the appalling stench of cold tobacco, the fetid breath of what is fake, forged, twisted. Enough to breed a ridiculous nostalgia for manure and raw milk. In Robert Musil's "Cacania"[30] (Austro-Hungary at the turn of the century), appearances were already gleaming luridly like spittle in sunlight. But let us speak no evil of appearances, they are all we have.

Where has eternity fled? Arthur Rimbaud knew the answer: *"Elle est retrouvée/. . ./C'est la mer allée/avec le soleil."*[31] Horizon, vanishing point, perspective. Do we still know how to open the windows of the infinite? Where has it gone, the reality for which the bell tolls, as Jean Baudrillard says with the joyful talent of despair? Are we entirely immersed in the ocean of pretense? Do we still have the energy necessary to inhabit our bodies, to live our lives? Has the crystal of experience been destroyed, or merely tarnished by the flashy proximity of surfaces? Or has it been replaced by the "real life" of television shows, as a Ming statue is replaced by a plastic vase?

Hand in hand, they walk along the boulevard. They watch an old lady tramp settle down for the night on a heap of garbage bags. A blinking electric sign sends flashes of light onto her flabby velvet hat and knotty forehead.

A passing car splashes their ankles with dirty water. In this city in distress, wild grass is already

growing between the pavement of the future.
   "To spend one night in your arms...."
   "Be quiet, oh please be quiet!"
   They resume their walk toward the métro.

The innermost truth of experience—womb of
creation and embryo of love—is not to be found
in lawyers' files, currency exchange rates, or
magazines. It has a few faithful seekers: lunatics,
artists, lovers. These stubborn characters keep in
tune with the shape of the sky. As the painter
Olivier Debré said one day on a radio program,
quoting Matisse: "When I paint, I see behind my
back." What destiny awaits these tenuous mysteries
on the art market?
   The very notion of "experience" has been
devalued by overuse in the "far out" Sixties and
Seventies. The naive illusion of that era was the
utopian belief that experience can be shared
collectively. Yet experience remains hidden, quite
naturally. Every individual is a world unto himself
or herself, every being a universe. From this point
of view, we are all different, radical strangers to
each other. What does unite us, however, is the
fact that each of us possesses a unique atmosphere.
The secret has gotten around! It is our uniqueness,
by its very existence, which connects us to the
universal—and not to the collective, which is
only its caricature, and which has proved to be a
boundless, desperate failure. And now from all
sides we are asked to deny our singularity. What

islands of peace survive the storms of media computerizing? Who can afford to contemplate a cherry blossom when the news is ablaze?

Homogeneity, the child of conformism, gains new ground every day on a planet where Japanese cartoons are shown in the West Indies and *Dallas* airs in Africa. The reign of artifacts, cosmetics, and glossy paper banishes unexplained thrills, sudden blushings, and passing angels to the antique store of "sensitivity." Yet they still happen. To deny their importance, to neglect their effect, to forget their existence, is to deny one's own self. This is no different from what people like Wim Wenders, Jean-Luc Godard, and other such Daedaluses are saying: isn't it strange to be living in a society where the essential is considered incidental?

A sincere and profound gesture can revive this crumbling world. In the manner of the Hebrew *tikkun,* where man's incessant activity repairs the shattered universe, it instills continuity into chaos, permanence into breathing. In the hubbub, a legato is sufficient, a sustained note, a lasting thought. From one key to the next, from one island to the other, the passage is free, without rough edges or regrets, in quiet certainty of the path. Cacophony fades away, a melody brings coherence. The world is made whole again. *Here I am.*

XIV

My "Map of the Ocean Floor" shows the naked
earth, stripped of her oceanic petticoats. How
beautiful she is! She hides nothing to the eye, her
calamitous pleated skin is tortured, gullied. She
is old and immodest: folds, abysmal trenches,
geological protrusions, dynamic ridges, concretions,
faults, crevices, heaps, burstings, fractures ... all
these scars are visible in her flesh, signatures left
by the ravages of immeasurable time. This is a
body, a very old body. The emerged lands appear
in yellow, the floor of the ocean is a mysterious
blue, side-lit by the cartographer in order to
emphasize its dramatic structure. The ancient
gestures of the earth are engraved in the traumatic
geology of her wrinkles.

The strangest thing is that these unfathomable
places have names. Indonesia draws an unfinished
necklace above the Wharton Basin and the Java
Trench. Between Alaska and Kamchatka, the
Aleutian Trench joins that of the Kuril Islands,
forming a ribbon-loop overshadowed by a 4,000-
meter drop, the Bering Abysmal Plain. Under the
volcanic pressure of her bowels, the earth carves
her history in her ravaged crust. *I dream:* this
earth is mine too, it also contains my untidy desk
and my postcards. No matter how hard I pinch
myself, I fail to see the relationship between these
two realities. *Perhaps my eyesight will be better in
another dream?*

A jagged spine runs the length of Greenland
from the Pole, splits Europe from America on its

way, circles Africa with a protective curve, works its way back up to Saudi Arabia and dives again into the breathtaking sub-Asiatic south, fends off India with a host of threatening sabers, then lengthens its meander toward southern Australia and eventually dissolves in the chaotic depths of the Pacific. Underneath Australia, by the way, the Furrow of the Diamantina etches a wound bordered by giant cliffs, opening onto the Abysmal Plain of the Great Bay. Colored in yellow, the high altitudes of terra firma—the Alps, the Himalayas, and other terrestrial heights—look second-rate compared to the fabulous oceanic ranges. My reason clouds, wandering through these immensities: opening the window, will I feel the ocean wind? In the heart of Paris? Come on!

I envy those who can decipher the handwriting of cataclysms, as my father could "tell" the exact age of the sectioned trees in the Forêt du Butard, thoughtfully calculating the number of rings in a stump bark, then confessing he might be off by a few years. I was not surprised by his knowledge; I already knew that shapes have their secrets and I was moved by the eloquence of these wounded surfaces. That my father should know the secret of trees seemed only natural to me. I had learned to read books; reading trees was surely not more difficult. On the other hand, a great mystery kept me busy: the idea that truth divides itself as it enters matter, that history does not fleetingly pass like the morning breeze, does not content itself with shaking the branches, but leaves signs, clues, entwined hearts carved in stone. What was it that stood at the border, the passage between my delight, the voice of my father, the destiny of the tree, and the lines in the naked wood? Is there an "escape" between silence and sound, as in a piano key? *What is the relationship between the love that makes my heart pound and the swirl of ink on the page as I write you this?*

I now know that love letters do get lost, or remain impossible to decipher, like the clay tablets of Minoan Crete, carved in a system of writing known as Linear A. No one ever has shed any light on this mystery. Yet the discovery made by Michael Ventris had given rise to great hopes: by testing the hypothesis that the language it coded was an archaic form of Greek, an idea until then considered pure folly by paleographists, he managed to decipher Linear B, a writing from a slightly later period.[32] But Linear A resisted all further attempts; the wall of meaning would not be shaken. I was indignant. It would have seemed only fair that humankind should be able to read its own messages.

Even at the time of these sweet educational excursions, the Forêt du Butard was starting to be reduced to a neighborhood. The leprosy of housing developments was turning the surviving trees into supernumerary garden ornaments. Nowadays, around the shooting lodge, the woods are in rags and tatters, patched with allotments; nearby, the highway sends a monotonous drone, stifling the silence as a crackling loudspeaker drowns out the shouts at an amusement park.

There it was: on the upper right hand side of

the map. In the suburbs of Paris, Seine *et* Oise, *département* 78, remember? A real *banlieue,* a trifle upscale but alive with tiny gardens, wisteria, forget-me-nots. In the late summer, clusters of seringa would burst feebly beneath my soles. Arco, our dog, was in the prime of life, with his incredible, shaggy black coat.

From my room on the allée du Butard, the highway sounded like a very faint bass note. The large trees leaned their antlers in front of my windows, the Collinet grocery store had fresh salads for sale, I careened around the narrow streets on my bicycle as far as the big intersection where I had gotten lost on the very first day. Since then, my sense of direction has not improved in the slightest. When in doubt, I ask my horse, ensuring that I get lost. I've never learned how to connect the map and the terrain, the stump of an elm tree and the cycle of the seasons.

I found the Map of the Ocean Floor in a wine bar on the Zattere in Venice, after a walk in the fog with Raphaël, my twelve-year-old son. The twilight spread a mantle of fatigue around our shoulders. At this far end of the city, the vista responds to the call of the distant seas which enliven the lagoon. Memories float in the evening air like long pink veils lifting up the damp fog.

Numb from the cold air and the beauty, we were grateful to enter the bar. The room was a few steps down, warmly furnished with wood and brass, like the living room in a ship at permanent anchor. The drinks were nice and warm, and above the bench, in a large mahogany frame, was the Map of the Ocean Floor. After walking along the canals of the moist, aquatic town, the appearance of the earth as dry land, entirely exposed to the contemplative eye, created a striking contrast. Its exotic beauty, its silent blue, answered today's question by directing our dreamy gazes toward the *proximity of depths.*

When several years later I found an identical copy of the map in the back room of a shop filled with miniature ships, I experienced again the wonder of that instant on the Zattere, of that fragile tête-à-tête with my son. And now Judith, who asks the right questions, has brought us still further into the mystery of the tiny streets where feelings unfold their misty wings. The beauty of Venice was devised to cover hatred and pain. Thus we love her dearly, as we love the earth and her submarine wrinkles. I keep the map at home, right in the middle of things. I appreciate its openness. Of course, the map is not the terrain. Often, it merely stands for absence. Other bars, other Venices, but on the same earth, under the same sky!

When my children were born, I entered the sun through the riddle of pain, and now the sun watches over them. The gestures of human beings, when they give birth to children, are not engraved in rock like ancient scripts. It is said they resemble the wake of ships at sea. They lodge themselves directly in the deepest folds of memory, in the sunken palaces of the miniature ocean.

XV

"Fundamentally, you are a monster: you find it perfectly normal to be loved."

It just slipped out. Another blunder. I ought to be muzzled. He lowers his head and looks at me, puzzled.

"Maybe you think I'm right?"

I lean against the white tiles of the Paris métro. I hold back the response that rises from my heart like a cluster of dragonflies. Of course you're right! Isn't it "normal" to love you? Don't all beings deserve to be loved? Why should you, of all people, be excluded from the community of the living beings who are worthy of love? On the other hand, to tell him he is right would be taken as unnecessary flattery. I dodge the question.

"Perhaps...."

As always, he pushes his advantage: "In any case, you're right. I am this monster you allude to: I do think it's normal for me to be loved, but I don't neglect doing a few things to make sure that I am. I must need to be loved."

He takes on a sheepish, guilty look. Bravely, I try irony: "In fact, you're sure of nothing." Then I pull out a trump.

"Obviously, you are putting your cards on the table, which has style. But I suspect your sincerity as being another one of your tricks. In any case, your conceit should get in the way of your plans."

"You know that is not true! On the contrary!"

"There's always an 'on the contrary' at strategic moments in conversations like this."

"Its the famous dialectic of "Madame de ...":
'I don't love you, I don't love you. ...' When I was
young I thought dialectic was wonderful. To my
everlasting regret I was never a Maoist, I was too
young."

"One is always too young for mental deficiency."

"I was lucky. I would have been easy prey for those
vampires. I always thought I was born stupid, which
proved I was smart."

"You see? I've never heard anyone so conceited!"

"For a long time, life bored me. My mind saw
only the banality of things. It began to change when
I understood death. I was relieved. There would be
an end to this story. I knew I would have to wait a
while to find out what death really was, but there
was no hurry. Instead, I had a lot more fun than
before. As Alfred Jarry said, death was invented for
the feeble-minded."

"In my opinion, death doesn't exist and neither
does the métro."

Ten minutes have passed as we stand dancing
from one foot to the other. There must be a mishap
up the line. Absorbed by our game of clever chatter,
we don't even smell the stink. (Dreamers gone astray
on a planet deprived of atmosphere.) In this corrupt
universe, everything exhales waste, even the moldy
green color of the subway tickets. Cheerful billboards
open fake windows onto the suburban maze. Their
dubious paradise is sometimes inspired by a flash of
genius: "You can find worse, but it costs more!"

On the opposite platform a closely entwined
couple exchanges sticky kisses on a yellow plastic seat
(what have become of public benches?). They are

glued together by the total surface of their skins, like Siamese twins. The guy's immense legs terminate in cowboy boots with spurs. A crest of red hair adorns his skull. The girl sits astride him, snakelike, hunched over his head, hair dripping, arms spread around his leather jacket. Her hands look as strange as the hanging paws of a dead fox on an old-fashioned wrap.

We ignore each other, two couples on opposite platforms. On one side a flutter of words, on the other a sinuous entanglement. Two worlds. In this métro station, the gestures (direction Clignancourt) and the words (direction Porte d'Orléans) are mutually exclusive. Between self-conscious chatter and idle necking, love has broken down, with all its subway cars.

XVI

"I say: air is the ghost of the world!" cried Judith, and it was not only an answer to her own question about the sky, but a declaration, a poetical manifesto. In the *Notebooks of Malte Laurids Brigge*,[33] Rainer Maria Rilke describes the traces left on the wall of a building by destroyed apartments: "You could see the inside.... The stubborn life of those rooms refused to be swept away. It was still there, hanging onto the nails still in place, digging into the fragments of floorplanks no wider than a hand which remained. It was still there, shriveled up in what was left of corners, where a touch of intimacy lingered on." The description goes on for several paragraphs, and one begins to picture the vanished rooms, the suspended beds, the dressing tables, the chairs, the mosquito nets, the perfume bottles, the dining table, the guests.... Remember when Mary Poppins and her charges begin to levitate during a tea party? Throughout his work, Rilke shows constant awareness of the void surrounding objects and defining their shape—just as the blank spaces separate words and give them meaning. He calls this void "atmosphere," contemplates it with awe, and notices that it alone captures memory. Like Cézanne, he wants to see *the depths of gray.*

Nothing else has ever counted for me but atmosphere, which gives life to instants and accompanies them in memory more clearly than electric signs. A yellow lamp, one evening in the living room of the big apartment. A stroll on the beach, barefoot in the sand. Where does atmosphere dwell? Inside the lamp? In the coolness of the sand? Or in the mind witnessing and creating them? In the phantom of the world, in my daughter's hair? I do not know, and I do not care. It is enough to take delight in it. Atmosphere comes from everywhere, from forever. It creates silence in noisy parties and a million noises in the dark countryside. It gives mystery to the stars. To peoples' faces, it imparts light, color, truth.

In front of my window, in Vaucresson, the swaying tree branches sketched thousands of fleeting stripes against the sky. On the terrace, in the summer, the red parasol was a cherry on the lawn; the buzzing of insects wove a carpet of sound (sometimes overcome by the celestial drone of an airplane, followed by its fading white plume). In the trunk of the tall elm tree, not yet felled by disease, a hollow space had taken the shape of a seat, an English armchair with wide oblique armrests. One was tempted to sit in it, but a patch of primroses had taken root there. At night I would go barefoot on the lawn and spin around the tree trunks until they grew dizzy.

The great flaw of modern buildings, however grand and colossal they may be, is their contempt for red parasols. The power of music stems from its ability to give birth to an atmosphere, to populate the world. *(One is enough: in your presence, even the atmosphere of the metro is no longer repulsive.)*

And a single note is enough, if the musician rightly weighs his attack. The shanai of Bismillah Khan, when it crosses the silence at the beginning of a raga, rends time with an unspeakable softness. It seems it has always been there, and it is bound to be endless.

The hero of Satyajit Ray's film *The Music Room* is reclining on his terrace when he hears the sound of the shanai flowing in from the neighbors' house. The shanai is a sort of Indian oboe; its slightly nasal sound is capable of an infinite variety of nuances, and it travels far. A feast is being prepared over there, in the other world, across the street. "Will the master go to the party?" asks the servant as he brings tea. The master extends his legs, wrapped in a plaid mohair, stretches and contemplates the universe: at the foot of the terrace begins the limitless Indian countryside. Not far off, a stream meanders. In late afternoons like this one, mist veils the generous colors of the summer. He contemplates the tragic beauty of India, which is also his own. Then he takes a sip of tea and answers the question with another question: "Do I ever go anywhere?"

Motion is an illusion, there is no other world: the party is also taking place on the terrace. The sound of the shanai has the power of awakening images. Such is the power of music, provided it has beauty. The world welcomes it, and music in turn makes the world more real, underlines its melancholy or its grace, causes young ladies to lighten their step. The heightened reality music brings about in things is tinged by the world it calls to life, the parade of images, dreams, fragments of thought drifting below the surface. Even the ideal listener, trained to maintain constant attention, is sometimes flooded by a host of associations. If he manages to keep them aside, in the margins of his mind, they will lose consistency, shed their contents, melt into listening. But their silent presence still enriches the music with an invisible trail of feelings.

And after the return to silence? Where does the atmosphere go? In a piece concluded with a sustained chord, how does the performer decide to stop the sound? Should he let it wind down and come to a stop, like a car in neutral? Most often, the pianist does not allow the sound to vanish by itself but lifts his hands off the keys, or his foot off the pedal: *Now. Silence.* It is an important decision, and an arbitrary one, no less than the previous choice of the initial attack, the irreversible event of the passage from silence to sound. In his way of coping with that kind of decision, the pianist reveals or betrays himself.

When he goes into the slow motion of a kata, which will last anywhere from thirty to forty minutes, Kenji Tokitsu seems to be immersed in his own concentration as in an ocean of slowness. We swim around him with our eternal beginner's water-wings and the room becomes an immense aquarium filled with a liquid that slows our movements and increases their power.

In the purified space of the dojo—varnished wood, protective shades, silences, breath—the atmosphere is enriched by an essential dimension:

the exchange between the internal pulsations and the perception of the partner's presence. *Ma* is what the Japanese call this evaluation of distance in combat, where the atmosphere forsakes the realm of mental play to create reality.

XVII

"There is no future left in music," said a music critic to my grandmother Esther in 1915, when she brought him her two boys for an appraisal of their musical capacities. He did not evaluate, he devalued; my father and uncle gave up their musical vocation. (According to the family legend, that is.) It so happened that music—namely, the piano—was to become for our family the garden next door, where you go for a stroll feeling that you could happily live there. It was a parallel world governed by beauty and joy, even on the darkest days.

My father found there a voluptuous refuge where he luxuriated in the intoxication of Schumann or Brahms, and from which he regretfully tore himself away. His sensitive, inspired playing was stunningly agile, though he remained but a knowledgeable amateur. No doubt he found in the garden of music, apart from pure musical enjoyment, the certainty of entering (within easy reach, at the tip of his fingers) an artificial dream vested with the permanence generally lacking in dreams, a dream capable of freeing him, for the duration of playing a ballad, from the ever-present "worries" that poisoned his life and would eventually, on a day of desolate bereavement, get the better of him.

For my father, music was a tenderly courted darling, a coquette who never yielded at the first caress, succumbing in order to withdraw, and whose smallest secrets fostered endless yearning.

"Truly elegant women never spend more than an hour getting ready to go out," he would say when he saw me exit the bathroom, red-faced from creams and masks, before a teenage party. "And I have known a few," he would add pensively, and I would envision, in a large forest lane lined with tall trees, a succession of fabulous belles miraculously painted and powdered.

Music has remained for me this impossible voyage to the time before my birth, a golden age, a stairway to the sky. For a long time I wandered down the side paths, not daring to *want* to play the piano. It then took me some time to admit that the universe of the piano was a blue mountain, and I wasn't even near it. Since my childhood I had sporadically practiced, but having never experienced the "depth of the keyboard," I remained on the surface of music.

With André Boucourechliev, keyboard practice revealed itself at last to be a way of exercising the ear. Listening to oneself—such is the pianist's duty. Technical skill does not serve virtuosity, it serves the ear. If the listening is really demanding, the fingers will perform. However, the capacity to listen is a skill in itself, a faculty which can be trained, as can memory. After several months of intensive effort I noticed that the growing exigencies of my ear gave birth to safer, more accurate gestures. An imaginary weight began to press upon my hands and forearms as if they were full of a liquid ready to flow through my fingers onto the keys and all the way into the strings, into the wooden heart of the piano. From time to time I witnessed a tiny miracle, and melted with pride like a mother when her baby babbles. The ear demanded a crystalline sound? The composer wanted a smorzando? The finger found the right angle, the right speed, the exact weight.

The glee associated with these small solitary feats is the secret foundation of practice. However, one must be wary of these isolated triumphs: they herald disaster. It is not enough to get it right once; the small miracle must be repeated at will. It must also, even as it becomes familiar, seek more refinements and question itself. What is technique but that which guarantees the repetition of the miracle and its development?

Time and again, after a few months spent on a particular score, I feel that I am reaching at last the foot of the mountain, a safe position where the real work of interpretation can begin and be heard by others. Then I remember that six months before I thought I had arrived exactly where I am today. And a year from now, I will once again rejoice at the sight of the mountain. Perfecting one's skill can be like jogging down a moving walkway going in the opposite direction.

A sudden light first blinds you. Then it shows you the world. Publishing houses are cluttered with unreadable manuscripts sent by people who think they know how to write since they know how to read. How about moving? We all think we know how to move, to raise an arm, to stand on one leg, to bend a knee. It is easy. In a t'ai chi class, all students—beginners or dedicated practitioners—perform the same exercises, the same sequence of gestures, for years. Their progress is measured by their ability to perform an identical form. The slightest motion of an arm, beyond its apparent simplicity, appears as complex and skillful as the brushstroke of a master calligrapher.

I wonder why we are unable to copy faithfully a single one of the teacher's moves. Yet we all think we've got it right! For months, for years, we are convinced we have perfectly understood this simple passage—a blow, a parry, a forward step. But a slight change in the position of the knee or elbow is sufficient to reveal the potential kick hidden in the advancing step, or the parry hidden in the kick. The tradition of martial arts encompasses coded meanings which are only brought to light after endless repetition.

Repeated again and again, the gesture gradually fills up; each attempt is loaded with the memory of the previous ones. Soon, the muscles recognize the way: a clearing opens up in the jungle of possible gestures as a mountain path deepens under hikers' footsteps. Gradually, the path of the gesture becomes visible, familiar, inescapable. It is engraved in memory, deep down where the stuff of the gesture lies dormant.

The remaining imperfections appear later on, once progress has taken place, once the correction has been made. While amending a posture, one suddenly perceives its previous defects: "The lower back was too stiff, the hands were too close to each other; I thought my shoulders were relaxed but only now are they really...." The form expresses and determines the multiple meanings latent in the gesture.

Thus the body, set in motion by the mind, exerts in turn its influence upon thoughts. In the instant when the arm finds its exact curve, the meaning of the curve is enriched with a new premise. And yet, until an experience creates it, the new meaning wasn't even an object of research. At each level, the students are temporarily satisfied with their progress. We wonder at our recently acquired sensitivity, at the stability of our balance, at our finer perception of details. After each stage (in every field, progress has stages), it will take us some time and sincere humility to question anew the recently acquired structure and to replace it by another, more efficient one.

Learning the art of piano playing is first and foremost a question of correcting errors. I sight-read a Mozart sonata. They seem so easy, these sonatas; beginners play them. Over the years I have enthusiastically made a hash of more than one. It sounds nice, the notes are right, more or less, but in fact I'm doing everything wrong: balance, accents, phrasing. It will take me months, perhaps years, to eliminate the mistakes, to clear the sonata of all the blunders with which I have burdened it, with the best of intentions. Fortunately, the more I work on it the less I tolerate errors.

Step by step, the quest for perfection becomes essential. As my ear grows more acute, my indignation rises at the sound of these residual blunders in the neurons of my digital memory. For mistakes can also be carelessly "learned" (misconceptions, faults in reading or interpretation) if one keeps repeating them. And they are stubborn! To get rid of them, you must start again from scratch.

If the physical sensation is right, the music will be beautiful. This is a fact, and a great mystery. When the touch is accurate, discordances resolve, angles are rounded, the impossible becomes possible. Opposites unite: motion and purpose, mind and body, gesture and instrument. Hit by the hammer, the string echoes in the pianist's bloodstream. An awkward move, a clumsy nuance, sets off a gruesome vibration which spreads through the fingers and wrists upward to the ears. Has any pianist not blushed, all alone, hitting the wrong key? First of all, the practice consists of eliminating unpleasant sensations. As I said, pleasure alone makes the rules. The privilege of learning is rarely celebrated with the glory it deserves.

It will take me months, perhaps years, to teach my fingers the paths to follow through this Mozart sonata. Years to learn how to add luster to this gruppetto, to unravel this passage which used to seem so easy and yet, once performed in the proper tempo, turns out to be as risky as a high-wire somersault. However, whatever it may seem to be, the ultimate goal is not victory over oneself but to *meet* oneself. Patience teaches that a dreary day can be redeemed by a tiny step forward—a better entrechat, a more successful javelin throw. Like desire, the spiral has no end.

Because the pianist aims for the unattainable absolute, he finds a way to capture its echo in the light touch of a chord. Years may go by before he dares to test a new resonance in a familiar piece or to smooth out a rough transition. All artists experience these secret joys, born of the momentary collusion between intention and act. The beauty of the gesture is an advertisement for paradise. Without this unending prospect and its whiff of the infinite, no art would ever be deepened; there would be no Budo masters, no pianists, no Chinese gymnasts.

XVIII

"Where I come from, we advise the person who has a hundred miles to go to look upon ninety as halfway!"[34] They all say this: when you begin to climb a mountain, the countryside is not the same as the view from the top. From here, the mountain-top is hidden by clouds—a Hokusai print. We know we shall never reach it. We don't even hope to; it would be like wanting to be elected President! It's not even an issue. We're too old, too Western, too urbanized. True followers devote several hours a day to their practice, which they began at the age of seventeen.

However, even for us, from our position in the foothills, the landscape is constantly changing. This makes it mysterious and alluring: we want to read the next chapter, we wonder about the view around the next bend. Despite our best efforts, we occasionally take the wrong path. Sometimes we try too hard. During a session of ri tsu zen, for instance, no matter how genuine the conviction that my shoulders are relaxed, time and time again they inch their way up as soon as my attention wavers. For months I praised myself for having found the correct position in another exercise, but I had failed to notice that the center of gravity was on the rear leg. Part of learning t'ai chi is over-coming such disappointments; the camera keeps moving, the landscape slides by.

To mean well is not enough. "You don't know how to study without constantly wondering: Will I succeed? Just wait patiently for whatever arises,"

Herrigel's teacher says to him after four years of daily effort. The very notion of "success" becomes problematic: a gesture which might seem correct to the layman appears "empty" to the trained eye of the master. Hitting the target is not enough. Herrigel tells of the time when he "successfully" hit the target thanks to an artificial shift in the position of his right thumb. He was expecting congratulations, but his master was furious. "My second shot seemed to me even better than the first. Then, without a word, the master walked over, took the bow from my hands and sat on a cushion, turning his back to me."

Accurate aiming is no artifice: it is his own self the archer sends into the center of the target. If the archer is absent from bow and arrow, the success of his shot becomes a failure, a parody. True accomplishment goes beyond skill and frees itself from the rules, providing the rules have been previously mastered. From up there, they say, the view is unobstructed all around.

I know a terrace on the roof of a parking garage in Montmartre, where Paris draws an immense circle around the expanse of tarred roofs; visitors stand there a long time in the wind, drawn by the nearness of space, transfixed by the swallows whirling spirals and graces, voluptuously listening to the city's breath while the setting sun fills their lungs with light.

In t'ai chi ch'uan, using the strength of one's muscles without connecting it to the central tanden would only be a false breakthrough. "Don't shake the boughs!" For the gesture to be full, the advancing arm must be connected to the center of the body and animated by it. Through this center, it is linked to all parts of the body. When the tree of the body with its swaying branches is experienced as a skin containing a liquid, it is easy to imagine the motion rippling, never weakening, from the tip of the toes to the face. A movement of the arm is then no more than the simple and quite natural consequence of a central motion which involves the whole body from the heels to the top of the head, passing through the belly, the chest, the elbows.

Heinrich von Kleist's puppets derive their gracefulness from the docility of their powerless limbs, responding to impulses from the center. "When the center of gravity advanced along a straight line, the limbs, on the contrary, designed a curve." Kleist describes in some depth this line drawn by the center of gravity, often straight, sometimes elliptic. It drags the arms and legs of the miniature dancers. He adds: "This line was also, seen from another perspective, a very mysterious thing. For it was finally nothing else than the path followed by the soul of the dancer." Puppets don't shake the boughs; they surrender. They have only a borrowed soul, that of the puppeteer. Kleist marvels at this paradox: the puppets, little golems, only achieve the perfect gesture insofar as they are not aware of moving. In this respect, they are strangely similar to the Zen archer who "shoots without shooting." But, says Kleist, and this is his real point, in order to reiterate the spontaneous grace of the marionette, to "revive a state of innocence," consciousness must "so to speak, sail across an infinity."[35] After this long aside, the master's abolished consciousness, having gone beyond rules, transcends the technique and reverts to elementary unconsciousness.

If one's upper body remains stiff, unconcerned by the separate action of the arm, the gesture might seem adequate but it remains empty, a caricature of what it might become. The internal void precludes efficiency. A gesture that is not attuned to itself has no effect on the outside world. The prerequisite of an efficient gesture is to be full— but full of what? Intention, vitality, energy? This fullness can only be described through metaphors (mental images), for it belongs to a realm of experience foreign to words.

To establish a certain continuity in purpose and therefore in movement—here is one of the first signs of tangible progress in t'ai chi ch'uan. But this continuity can only be created once the task of memorizing the formal sequence has been fulfilled; intimate knowledge of the form enables one to anticipate subsequent moves and thereby execute them without hesitation or surprise. It has taken us months, in some cases years, to memorize the slow choreography of the "morning kata."

In school we are taught a few poems and speeches. But almost nothing is done, in the life of ordinary people who are not dancers even if they practice sports, to develop the specific memory which stores the movements of the body. It so happens that this bodily memory has a structuring power for the psyche: it changes a disjointed succession of gestures into a mobile narration, it carries meaning. The same applies, naturally, to musical memory, which is the binder, the rich soil of interpretation. (However, there is one difference: a tune, for reasons which have yet to be discovered, seems much easier to memorize than a sequence of gestures.)

And memorizing is not the most difficult part. Chances are never equal, but while repeating the same gestures a dozen times a week, everyone eventually succeeds. The memory of the form must be engraved simultaneously in the limbs and in the area of rational thought which provides points of reference, chapter headings ("beginning of fourth section ... oh, yes, here, hands like clouds, watch the position of your foot ... twice only in this section ... no, the diving comes later ..."). Gradually, in the new lighting brought forth by the blending of the two memories, each gesture finds its place in relation with the others, becomes familiar. There are those one happily returns to, those from which one recoils (must I really bend down so deeply in order to turn?), those one "gets right" the first time, those which have given us so much trouble and which, today, seem easy....

In the global architecture of the kata, articulations appear gradually, like blanks in a written page covered with continuous letters. They add punctuation and syntax, elucidate, clarify. The same thing happens when studying a sonata. Blurred passages grow accurate, masses become clear, leitmotivs become manifest, and each bar, each fragment of the musical text, begins to exhale its own personality like an open perfume bottle. The growing awareness of the hidden structure of a musical piece (or of a kata) emerges along with the delight it brings.

Repetition. Here is the difficult part. Is there a way out of this dreary flatland? Without repetition, there can be no scenery, no mountain, no perfume, no real fun. Repetition is the royal approach to learning; it stands guard at the entrance to the temple like an army of officials to be saluted one by one. It may seem fastidious, especially in a culture fascinated by novelty and cheap thrills. Repetition used to symbolize slavery, the tedious gestures of the chain gang. It is the ordeal and ultimate test in any process of learning. Nonetheless, as a bit of practice will prove, repetition is an illusion; actually, the gestures of human beings (unlike those of puppets) never repeat themselves. It is impossible to imitate oneself exactly. Repetition escapes monotony through tiny variations in weight, distance, intention, intensity, or, as Robert Pirsig would say, Quality. For the hundredth time I climb this chromatic scale with its impossible fingering. Each time the attack is slightly different, weak spots change places, the intensity of the crescendo varies. My secret hope is that one day, perhaps, these tiny differences between two strokes of the brush will be chosen, mastered, freed from the rules, relevant to the music alone.

But the most difficult of all is neither memorization nor the repetition which serves it. The most difficult is that which seems easy.

Slowness, for instance. One believes it is easier to move slowly than fast, just as one imagines it is less tiring to go down a staircase than to climb it, and less trying to play pianissimo than to play forte. Just try to walk two meters in five minutes, passing from one foot to the other without stopping at all and with arms raised!

Imitation. It also seems easy. What could be simpler, on the face of things? Even babies can imitate! When I was seven or eight, as I was reveling behind locked doors in the pleasures of Offenbach's *La Belle Hélène*, I was totally convinced I could perfectly copy the light soprano in Hélène's famous aria: "*Dis-moi, Vénus, quel plaisir trouves-tu/A faire ainsi cascader, cascader ma vertu...*" ("Tell me, Venus, why you so enjoy making my virtue cascade, cascade...").

Misdirected common sense holds that it is easy, even pointless, to imitate someone else's gestures. Generally speaking, our novelty-struck culture values creative activities over imitation, which it considers at worst as plagiarism, at best as a provisional stage in a process of liberation. We assume imitation and creation are opposite poles, magnets pushing each other away. But in opposing the two, lovely faces versus lively minds (instead of trying to bring them together), our society produces many a lovely empty head, thus widening the gap in the transmission of ancient wisdom. Artistic or intellectual creation cannot be conceived of without tutelage from a lineage of masters. There can be nothing really new without a clear awareness of the experience handed down to us from old, even if one hopes to destroy it. This explains why imitation is the basic principle of any teaching. It takes care of the essentials, of the learning of words, expressions, gestural codes, rites of love. Yet in our schools imitation is despised, together with memorizing, and for the same reason: it is too "easy"!

For decades, to its everlasting regret, the West scoffed at Japan for its uncanny ability to imitate Western technology, as if imitation were a railway siding, a parrot's skill. In interpreting a kata, the line does not stand between imitation and creation but between clumsiness and ability. In other words, an artist's renown has no weight when set against his absolute dream. A 1993 exhibition at the Louvre of copies of Old Masters by their successors magnificently illustrated the passage from imitation to inspiration. There is no better way to learn—no better muse—than the faithful imitation of a simple gesture: a brushstroke, an arpeggio, a parry. The teacher brings his arm forward, I do the same. But I have neglected the position of my shoulder, which is too far back; as for my elbow, it's sticking out in the wrong direction. It is from *within* that the gesture must be imitated, in its direction, its meaning; if the meaning is clear, if the movement is full, both elbow and shoulder will fall into place on their own.

The difficulty stems from the difference between the image of our body as perceived by our feelings, our habits and fantasies, and its external image as reflected in a mirror. Of course each of us is blind to our own imperfections, and we are only too aware of other people's flaws. Why doesn't she bend her knees a little more? Why does he move his right foot so far forward? Obvious mistakes are first noticed in others. Where our own weaknesses are concerned, our vision tends to blur. This is the way we are: we think that to wish is to achieve. We try our best, so we're bound to succeed. Dead wrong! Self-criticism is in order! Beware of the ego!

Imitation of the teacher's gestures is instructive precisely because of its imperfections. One can spot a beginner from his blindness to his own errors. He doesn't see that his knees are stiff; he's convinced that he is doing exactly the same thing as the teacher. Progress means becoming aware of one's mistakes; to some extent, they can never be cured. Each of our katas is a draft, more or less scribbled, of the ideal kata represented by the teacher's movements. The approximations differ according to morphology, vitality, concentration. But mistakes are also personal and "packed with meaning."[36] In mathematics, as in t'ai chi ch'uan or piano, our mistakes reflect our specific style, that undefinable singularity which makes our handshake as recognizable as a voice, or a signature.

When trying to play pianissimo, the apprentice pianist supposes that to lighten his touch he must relax his fingers. He is the victim of an illusory mimesis between goal and tool. A similar confusion turns flexibility into flabbiness, intensity into excess speed, strength into rigidity. The result is a music full of holes. Seeking a gentle sound is no reason to play with relaxed fingers! On the contrary: only firm phalanxes allow control over intensity and tone, and thus over the pianissimo. This primal discovery needs to be constantly rebuilt. What seems paradoxical becomes self-evident, even instinctive, as soon as the firmness in the fingers is allied to another flexibility that flows from the wrists and the back, giving buoyancy to the elbows and creating a general feeling of well-being.

Discoveries follow one another. The sensations created by the gesture in progress send messages back in turn, allowing the gesture to expand, find its curve, go into orbit. At the height of artifice, movement becomes natural and flows from its source. "I have for master my heart, my heart has for master my eye, and my eye has for master Mount Hua." What may seem a paradox to us was for Shitao another expression of "The Single Brushstroke."

Without hoping to climb Mount Hua, we find that the dynamic of traveling is an end in itself, sustained by the pleasure of overcoming obstacles. As years go by, some gestures which seemed impossible to perform just happen calmly. What has been acquired consolidates, the memory of sequences, the exact bend of the knee, the position of the foot. Each new stage opens up an additional mountain pass, a canyon waiting to be crossed, a tormented landscape waiting to be flattened.

How frustrated we are, we amateur musicians, barred from the highest, doomed to feed on crumbs from the feast! Beggars of sound, loitering at the gates of the kingdom, a crowd of nobodies! A famished diaspora of starving, bashful, wretched creatures! Unable to accompany a singer on the spot! Unable to sight-read! Unable to play one single piece to the end without a mistake!

Amateurs, knowing that they count for nothing in the realm of music, are kept humble. In fact, they are not second-rate suitors (as the ambiguous word "amateur" would have us believe), but first-rate lovers, transfixed and amazed at the permanence of their passion. The etymology is clear: amateurs are those who love (Latin, *amare,* "to love"). That is their good fortune, their talent, their weakness. They are infatuated with music. As Princess Bibesco wrote one day to Marcel Proust, "the debtor, in love, is the one who loves." Being loved brings secondary pleasures — pride, comfort, power — whereas the flame of given love lights the dark corners and makes life more beautiful. Amateurs feel an intense gratitude for music because she constantly provides them new reasons to love her. That is why they play with her, stroke her, flatter her, hoping she will yield more of herself. But how she resists!

Music is an addiction, a lamp illuminating the texture of existence. The amateur is instinctively faithful to the original glimpse which made it clear that his life could never be without music. One day a fragment of the real universe was handed to him. Two *Ländler* by Franz Schubert, Vinteuil's "little phrase" in Proust's novel, a fork ringing on a crystal vase. In his novel *Job*, Joseph Roth sends the harmonics of this crystalline sound echoing like bells of destiny throughout the life of his hero.[37]

Held captive by his childhood dreams, the amateur retains the freshness of his lost future and feels an absurd sort of pride in "knowing what music is all about." He tries old pianos in empty drawing rooms, always ready to disappear underground if a "real" pianist should pass the doorway. His insatiable desires keep him happily busy.

A nightmare. I am giving a concert in the garden. The audience settles on garden chairs. They whisper, waiting for me. I begin to play. I make a great effort to push my fingers one by one into the keyboard. They sink into the keys but produce no sound. Are my fingers too weak? Is there something wrong with the piano? Have I gone deaf? Has sound ceased to exist? I don't know what to do—continue the piece or start again? I start again. Nothing happens. Total silence, as in a convent school refectory. I start to feel hot. I notice a woman standing up and going toward the woods in the background. I play on, sweating heavily. People get up and leave, looking indignant, and the utter silence remains.

Whenever I recount this old, recurring dream, someone invariably makes the point that all pianists, even the greatest, have such dreams. The fear of failure is the reverse side of desire. Each of us has a host of personal ghosts, soft spots, and scars. The point of music lessons is that they convert the fear of inadequacy into the joy of serving music.

One could draw up a list of amateur character types, dividing them according to their interests, their nostalgia, their outlandish dreams. The sheepish amateur secretly performs his little piece, hoping that his soul may be heard through his flabby fingers. He blushes while admitting his hobby, as if confessing an illicit liaison. "Yes, I do mess around a little on the piano. . . ." The pretentious amateur massacres a Bach fugue with conquering inaccuracy. The shy amateur barely touches the keys, frightened to try their weight. The enthusiastic amateur sight-reads Schumann's *Kreisleriana* at a hundred miles an hour, missing every other note. The nostalgic amateur, having abandoned music, feels in turn abandoned by her.

At times, the amateur is seized by an impulse. It is early morning, after a party, his mind is clear and calm. This is the risky hour of *why not?* He places his hands on the keyboard. A little melody rises, but soon flickers like a flame in the breeze. After a while, he is obliged to admit to himself that his fingers feel numb, his gestures are faltering, his control over his muscles is weak, his reading of the score is slow. He lacks technique, the mother of all freedom! *But the birds are already up and beginning their chirping. A sob bursts in his*

chest, an overflowing grief contrasting with the light
of dawn, and his tears celebrate his homecoming to
that other dimension, that splendid space-time
where playing and dreaming are unhindered.

There are also, or so I am told, truly serene
amateurs, free of inhibitions and fears, who go
their merry way through inexhaustible thickets
of the piano repertoire. They are explorers,
insatiable readers. Musical literature is filtered
through their well-tempered keyboard, they
decipher Beethoven quartets transcribed for the
piano as ordinary people read the newspaper. Yet
I suspect that they still harbor, deep in their secret
garden, a little stream of nostalgia for the experience
of the perfect gesture.

There are millions of amateur musicians and
this ever-increasing number has spectacular effects
on record sales and concert attendance. The music
lover differs from the amateur in that his passion
is satisfied with the simple serenity of listening.
The music lover has no cause for disquiet, he has
set no goal. The amateur, ever impetuous, has never
given up his impulse to *touch* music.

The solitary amateur makes the mistakes of any
autodidact. He drowns defective legatos with excess
pedal, trips on the same scale for years, accelerates
in the crescendo. In a word, he stagnates. He knows
well that by staying *in touch* with music, he remains
faithful to himself. But only those who ask for help
and advice resume their climb toward the peak.

Of course it is too late, time has run out; the
adult amateur will never reach the top and in any
case, there are other tasks to attend to. You have

no illusions as you start working your way up through the scales once again. But how beautiful is the road! Each progress made in the quality of sound, in accuracy, in interpretation, feels like that hairpin turn in the road which unveils a new horizon. Day after day, you experience the pleasure of improvement as a reward in itself, one that offers ample compensation for the retreat of the mirage. You seek excellence, but do not complain about being so far from it. As you make progress, music speaks more clearly to you but it becomes even more unattainable, even more enticing. Like the Sunday skier contemplating the champion's inspired christianias etched in fresh powder on the slopes of the Matterhorn, you feed your dream with awe at the sight of the "real" pianists.

In this lifetime, you may never experience the ecstasy of sweeping down Schumann's snowy arpeggios in one of those effortless cascades where each sound finds its proper place in the musical phrase, where nothing interrupts the flow. The more you face your own limits, the more you look up to the perfection of the masters, the more sensitive you become to a magic phrase, a subtle ritardando, a swift flutter of trills. It *can* be done! Perfection is a myth, a call from afar. The amateur is content to know this. He is primarily a philosopher, for want of being something else.

XIX

A kiss, a jump, a blow—are they fleeting nothings or meaningful scratches on the walls of time? Does not motion pertain to every human activity? "Man is fundamentally active and can never remain motionless," says the master swordsman Itusai Chozanshi.[38] Does not the act of writing require the hand to move? And when we think, do we not need to scratch our head, rub our nose? Speaking makes our lips (and hands!) move. Singers may appear to be just standing there, but are in fact performing a series of internal gestures, calling on larynx, chest, stomach, back. Are these gestures any less real for being invisible?

Where is the limit between stillness and motion? At what tick of the clock does a gesture begin? Immobility changes into motion in discrete increments, just as night becomes day, as silence becomes sound. In ri tsu zen, once the pain in your thighs has lessened, immobility stops tormenting you when you realize that you are, in fact, constantly moving, breathing, living. Your heart beats, you twist a shoulder, straighten your neck, relax your face: immobility is a mere abstraction. It has no more existence than repetition or silence. We are the seat of a perpetual motion, of intense activity, way beyond mere blood circulation or the rumbling of organs; this is the hidden throbbing of life.

In the gracious immobility of an antique bas-relief, the archeologist Norbert Hanold, the absent-minded hero of Wilhelm Jensen's *Gradiva*,[39] discovers the breathtaking beauty of a woman's forward step, as one sees light from a distant star. "There was something about her, something not often found in the statues of antiquity, the natural, simple grace of a young girl which gave rise to the impression that she was overflowing with life. Perhaps this came from the way in which her movement was portrayed? Her head was slightly bent forward, in her left hand she held her dress slightly raised, its extraordinary little folds rippling over her from the nape of her neck to her ankles, where you could just glimpse her sandalled feet. Her left foot was leading and her right prepared to follow, touching the ground with its toes alone while her arch and heel were raised almost vertically."

Fascinated by this erect pose, Hanold embarks upon dubious podiatric investigations and questions his friends about the feet of walking women. He feels he must grasp the link between this improbable posture and the entire step of which it is just one split-second part. And yet he need only open his eyes; he dreams of Gradiva as she was in ancient times, alive and striding along the streets of Pompeii just moments before the eruption of Vesuvius, but if only he noticed, he could find the same step in his nextdoor neighbor Zoé Bertgang when she passes by. At her window, a canary sings. He has known Zoé since childhood, when they used to play together. And yet so profoundly has he repressed the memory of those disturbing games that he no longer recognizes Zoé, now a young woman, when she walks down the stairs or passes on the street. Instead, he dreams of Gradiva, "disappearing along the tiled sidewalk, frightening a lizard with its moiré coat of gold and green."

This delightful novel, which Freud examined in a long commentary, tells the story of a dead soul returning to life. Absorbed in old stones, Norbert Hanold is absent from this earth, a foreigner to his own wishes, unconscious of his destiny. Through a motionless statue—a *dream of stone*[40]—he rediscovers mobility, grace, longing. Thanks to the beauty of a gesture, he tastes life again. The step of Gradiva sauntering through the buried streets, once imagined, is unforgettable. Jensen brings good news;[41] he proves that the art of writing, no less than a bas-relief or a photograph, has the power to capture movement.

The early photographs of the "hysterics" in La Salpêtrière hospital in Paris at the end of the last century illustrate in a most puzzling way the ambiguous relationship between stillness and motion.[42] The invention of photography seemed to produce a way to reiterate instantly the feat of Gradiva's anonymous sculptor: "catch her from life as she passed by in the street." At last, human-kind was able to capture motion in full flight. Thus the photographer Regnard was able to take photo after photo of Augustine, one of the famous "hysterics" of the Charcot era. The question is, how does one imprint a drifting soul on plates of wet collodion?

A series entitled "Passionate attitudes" shows Augustine in her nightshirt on a bed, her hair undone, beside herself. Here she seems ecstatic;

there she pleads, sticks out her tongue, rolls her eyes, petrified. Another print captures her at the onset of a fit of "hystero-epilepsy"—her arms are tied behind her back, her chest is constricted by a straightjacket, her mouth is open, one can almost hear her scream of terror. But here is the catch: this ecstasy, this torment, these cries were staged. *Tutto preparato!* These "scientific" snapshots were the result of painstaking rehearsals, capable of trying the patience of any modern fashion model.

In the era of the Kodak Instamatic—and, more generally, of instant connections—we tend to forget that photographic art, in its early stages, required lengthy exposures during which the model had to remain totally still. The photographers had set up a whole laboratory in La Salpêtrière: "A full-scale operation: platform, beds, screens, and black, dark gray, and light gray backdrop curtains, head supports and brackets...." How long did Augustine have to hold the particularly painful grimace of Plate XXVI? Fifteen seconds? Two minutes? "Look at the sweep of terror which seems to pass over the face of Rosalie; it is not at all a brief passage, but rather a concentrated timespan, an actual 'contraction of the face.'" The temporal burden of primitive technology prevented these photographs from fulfilling their official purpose, which was to reveal to the doctor the hidden truth of hysteria. On the other hand, the lengthy exposure, because it obliged the "hysterics" to exaggerate the theatrical side of their symptoms, has turned these images into excellent snapshots of the medical obsessions of the time. The paradox of the setting is perverse. By distorting the gestures in order to make them more explicit, the long exposure discarded the reality which gave them meaning and which the plates were meant to reveal. The genuine gesture does not attempt to impress the viewer. What makes it unquestionable is its innocence.

For this reason, Augustine's feelings, her ecstasies and terrors, still remain shrouded in mystery. All we know is that in the end she ran away from la Salpêtrière, as Babar and Celeste escaped from the circus, in the middle of the night.

XX

Music and katas tell stories. Everyone can make up their own.

The first four bars of Mozart's *Sonata in B-flat major* (K570) evoke for me a man taking long strides with his arms wide open (seven alternate minims and crotchets). He comes towards me and asks a question. It's an *overture*, in the strong sense of the word. In order to make these seven notes dance (they are played in unison by both hands), in order to lift these seven veils, the pianist's hands must ally strength and flexibility, eagerness and restraint. On the perfection of this weighing depends the voicing of the question: *"Do you love me? Are you glad to see me?"*

In t'ai chi ch'uan, the fullness of a gesture also depends on the weighing and harmonizing of contradictory tensions. On the seventh note, the fingers regretfully quit the last F played in the treble, leaving a question mark in the air. The hand soars into the suspension which precedes the answer: a little melody in quavers, appeasingly conclusive, repeated once before it finally resolves. It is a curtsey, expressing the joy of meeting. A delightful gruppetto launches the bounding ascension to the dominant F, then a whirling descent to the basic key of B-flat. Back to earth, gently and smoothly. Back to the love chamber, after a stroll. *"The answer is yes."*

It's a lot of fun: a succession of *yesses*. Why is this *yes* for me the very essence of Mozart? *On vacation in Biarritz with my parents, I was eager to*

*visit, as they had promised, a mysterious place
called the "Chamber of Love." My father parked the
car at the edge of the beach and we walked toward
the sea. It was raging that day, the waves were high,
blue flames shooting their tongues of foam toward
the heavy clouds. It was dramatic, but I was still
waiting for my parents to take me to the famous
Chamber of Love I had so often dreamed about.
Surprised by my request, they exclaimed, in unison,
"But this is it! This is the Chamber of Love!"*

*So this was love—this dark splendor, this ocean
turmoil, this overcast sky. I assented. Yes, this is it.
The Chamber had the infinite for a ceiling, sand for
a floor, my parents' bodies for pillars. I thought I
could understand how a beach could be a chamber.
I saw space sing. You just added walls, windows,
shadows, and magnificent loved ones. I was secretly
disappointed, but I understood: love needs open
spaces in which to spread out; it gives everything
away in a single gesture when the moon is full, and
it makes children grow.*

*Later, along with the blue haze of the Rockies, I
packed the Chamber of Love away in the secret trunk
where I keep my cherished illusions from the past.*

Technical mastery relies on mental images to
find its balance between weight and grace. The
questions "Do you love me? Are you happy to see
me?" serve the same function as the beach ball:
they encourage the gesture. Incorporated within
technique, mental images expand the technique.

No longer automatic, it embodies the growth of musical sensitivity. But its goal remains its own transcendence; in perfecting your technique, you prepare yourself for the moment when technique will cease to give you orders and begin to serve the music directly. When this goal is attained, even for a brief instant, technique vanishes, along with the fingers, the score, the piano, and the pianist. Only music remains.

Mental images, which are a part of technique, are also bound to dissolve. "Here, light a star ..." wrote Boucourechliev on my score of Bach's *Partita in C Minor*, just before the two-voice fugue. These stars are located on the peaks of a long climb; with each ascension, the demisemi-quavers touch the sky, like the streetlamp lighter in *Le Petit Prince*, circling around his tiny planet with his flame. For years now, whenever I play this partita the little man appears, always at the same bar, and disappears a few bars later. Perhaps he lives there?

He is as discreet as the lady who lodged with her six children inside a giant shoe. A ladder enabled them to climb over the edge and go out for walks. They wandered all around the floor of my room, conquering new territories. One of them got his feet entangled in the hair of my doll. Like Percinet in his prison, I struggled in vain to coax them back into their home.

These imaginary scenes are fleeting, destined to vanish of their own accord once their mission has been fulfilled, to let others take their place, yielding to the music. Some are linked to the score, to the reading. If you play by heart they fade away, as new ones appear. Some have a gift for lingering on, persuasive as a note of perfume in a lady's wake. Linked to a certain bar, a theme, a modulation, they pull along behind them a long series of mental landscapes which call out to each other. They also break up and blur as time goes by, leaving bits of memory clinging to the branches of the melody like cotton on a carding comb. Later, perhaps, when music has filled the entire horizon, images may become useless. One never knows.

Sometimes the thoughts associated with a strain of music or a passage of t'ai chi ch'uan have no relation to the gesture being made. They come bumping up against it like lost birds, detached from their home base, lost in a world in which they don't belong. They're leeches, parasites. They interfere. They carry trite messages from the ordinary world. They have no reason to be there, in this music, in this kata. They're a swarm of midges, the hissing and crackling of a bad phone connection, the babble of the banal.

For example, when I practice Chopin's first *Étude* (op. 10), at the end of the second page I am often visited by the disturbing silhouette of X. I see no relationship between that unpleasant person and this magnificent *Étude*, which arches its back like a cat when stroked. X's entry on the scene of my consciousness, which I had hoped to focus solely on the width between my fingers and their agility, feels like a knife scraping across a plate. Fortunately it skims the surface of my thoughts, like a scrap of paper dropped by the wind, a dead leaf on a bench: my gestures are in no way affected by the interference. In the real world, the *Étude* continues to raise its magical waves. After a few bars, X's face blurs like an over-exposed photograph, then disappears. Alas, he still turns up at the same page, for no reason, like the Canterville ghost: old and ridiculous, with rusty chains and strips of rotting flesh clinging to his skeleton.

The distinction between parasitical thoughts and fruitful evocations is easily made. The latter are the result of concentration, they pertain in some way to the music or to the kata. These parasites have nothing to do with art or motion; like swallows, they circle aimlessly, madly screeching. They must be chased away ruthlessly.

To each of us, Mozart's sonata tells a different story, entirely visible in the gestures of the pianist. You could almost hear it on a silent keyboard. It would be fine music for the deaf. Like us, the deaf hear their thoughts in the silent music of motion. So they love music in their own way, for the sight of it. In Nicolas Philibert's film *The Country of the Deaf,* they even pretend to play a quartet, just to get the feel of it. Those who cannot hear at all, who depend upon gestures to communicate (the spoken word, when they manage—at the cost of great effort—to master its usage, remains for them a foreign language), know how great is the wealth of meaning conveyed by gestures. From this point of view, we are illiterates compared to the deaf. We are not aware of one one-hundredth of the potential messages of our gestures.

This corporal illiteracy is manifest every time Kenji Tokitsu proposes a new kata. To reproduce a simple succession of moves without a mistake is extremely difficult for us sedentary city-dwellers. To memorize the sequence might require months of patient repetition. And the result? After years of practice, we are still learning the alphabet.

There is an easy explanation for our incompetence. Nothing has prepared us for the concept that everyday gestures might be philosophical exercises. No one has advised us to pay attention to them, to stop viewing them as chores, to start loving them and perfecting them. In beauty classes young women are taught to make a good impression, not to be one with their gestures. In sports, motion serves the performance, when it should be the other way around. In our society, exercising the memory of gestures seems out of place, and learning poems by rote is definitely out of fashion.

This may be why for many years I considered gestures subordinate to real life, mere tools. At the piano I remained on the surface, hoping to reach the music directly without giving much thought to what my hands were doing. I considered physical disciplines less noble than the art of language, which I viewed as the exclusive purview of knowledge.

The excessive importance given to the intellect and its words, over the body and its gestures, is still one of the basic clichés of our mental universe, even if we are fascinated by sports. Questioning it is a real challenge, an experience of limits. This absurd hierarchy only survives thanks to another even more durable cliché, the obsolete and illusory separation of mind and body.

This is something anyone can experience. As soon as we try to move in a conscious manner, we become aware that the success of this attempt relies on the flow of breath through arteries, lungs, and muscles. Breath makes its way through every one of our acts, through our very words. (The lethal pleasure of cigarette smoke curling its way through our lungs is an absurd confirmation of the vital importance of breath.) Throughout our life we breathe unconsciously. Yet it is possible, by virtue of a strange privilege, to control this automatic flow, to shape it and direct it. In this way breathing is animated by the spirit, however automatic it may seem. But the loop never closes, since the body also acts upon the mind, and breath returns to its source. After a class of t'ai chi ch'uan our mood is clear. Something has shifted. The clarity of our thoughts is a manifestation of the beauty of the gesture.

XXI

Blink, scratch your nose, rub your eyes, tidy your hair, adjust the strap of your handbag, bite your fingernails. Rilke describes Rodin's sketches as "strange documents of the instantaneous," a collection of careless, unimportant gestures made by models unconscious of being watched. Their great merit is their spontaneity, freed from the narcissistic preoccupation of the model posing for the painter. Hence, their revealing power.

Most of our gestures are automatic, at least those which weave the cloth of life, filling the chinks in time, the intervals of waiting, the uninspired moments. According to Rilke, Rodin was the first to capture the unconscious motion: "The air we breathe is written on our faces." His fragmented drawings, taken from life, like the antique Gradiva, might be the artistic analogy of Freud's "Witz"—revealers, peepholes, visions.

Are we not, most of the time, absent from our own gestures? How many small moves do we perform mindlessly during a day, without content or aim? Who guides these actions, if we don't give them attention, if we are not there? Are you present in each one of your steps? And in your embraces? This time it is the later Rilke, the poet of the *Duino Elegies*, who asks the question:

> *Lovers, sufficient unto each other*
> *It is you whom I question about what we are.*
> *You say you embrace. Are you sure of it?*[43]

"On my way to school one day, in the springtime light, I walked along with the dark spot of my shadow on the dirt path above the rice fields, and I tried to walk truly, to be present in each step, in vain."[44] This boyhood experience was to become an essential issue for Kenji Tokitsu and determine his commitment to the martial arts. In similar circumstances a French adolescent would have voiced an anguished inquiry about the rationality of words, the existence of God, or his own existence. "Why am I me?" asks the little girl as she falls asleep. "Why, oh why, when I was born, was it me and not somebody else?" *(As the Indian sage says, since life is a dream, I was not born and will never die.)* Soon, the child understands that the answer is not available: one has to look inside.

However, Tokitsu's question not only brings the germ of an answer (is that not the role of questions?) but of an instrumental, matter-of-fact answer. Metaphysical awe is converted into research. Reflexive consciousness merges into action. The *why* retreats behind the *how*. Anxiety is lifted by creating a technique. The question, *How can I really be myself?* is instantly followed by, *What can I do about it?* Behind the question *how,* calling for immediate practical answers and lifelong reflection, the ontological vertigo begins to fade. I don't know who I am; we'll look into that later. But for the time being, how shall I manage to truly live my life, be who I am, eat what I eat, walk when I walk, hear what I listen to, see what I see, savor my feelings, my sensations, enjoy the world's and art's creatures, make them mine? Is there, by any chance, a task more important than to live one's own life?

How can I unite the expression of my feelings with their inner truth? Is it possible to overcome that instinctive cheating which causes us to act other than what we really are, makes us foreign to our gestures as if they were someone else's, prompts us to look for truth in its caricature? How to be sure we are not half-kissing, mechanically stroking, laughing too loudly, simulating emotions? How not to doubt my own sincerity when I smile, when I flirt? How can I fill my gestures, make them real, harmonious, efficient? How can I give the present moment—the only reality—the attention it deserves?

These elementary questions are rarely asked in our world, subjected as it is to the dictatorship of clocks and appearances. The image has drifted away from its anchor, empty communication has replaced the fullness of words, packaging comes before content and existence before essence. We are threatened by entire universes of virtual reality worthy of the film *Total Recall* (based on a book by Philip K. Dick): carried away into a world of his choice, the customer beats a path through the jungle with his machete. Naturally, everything is fake, the leaves brushing against his forehead, the birdsong, the machete, the humid tropical sky, the buzzing, the insect bites.

The feeling is there, *total*, perfect, but it is connected to no reality save that of electronic circuits. These virtual universes will soon be to the cinema what the cinema is to painting. From one invention to the other, what first appears as vivid as a hallucination becomes each time as safe as a fake window. The advantage of artificial reality is that you can touch up the photo, choose the color of the sky, the shape of the clouds, invent the film in which you are the hero. The purified reality of the virtual world is designed to ensure total and purified enjoyment, in the absence of objects. Nothing is there, apart from a subject bombarded with artificial stimuli. Not a soul alive in these parts of the world. "Love is not loved."[45]

In the hustle-bustle of modern cities, how can we find the calm and perseverance vital in order to give full attention to what is going on: a chat on the phone, the tide of cars on the boulevard, a murmured confession, the warmth of your skin?

To be here tonight, far from you? On my untidy desk my tired thoughts are stranded. I keep watch on my computer screen: black-on-gray words that never cease being born, little angels expelled from a dream without a dreamer. It is summer. Absence also has its music. The ventilator sends a cloud of gnats spinning to the cone of my lamp. I crush them with the tip of my finger; nothing remains but a tiny green mess.

XXII

"I want to examine this problem a little, to see if in that strange separation between what man is and what man does, we may find a clue as to what the hell has gone wrong in this damned twentieth century." This is Robert Pirsig's purpose in *Zen and the Art of Motorcycle Maintenance*, an initiatory journey along the back roads of America. Pirsig manages, and it is quite a feat, to make his readers share his passion for nuts and bolts.

Logically, the search for wholeness in gestures should erase the usual hierarchies we establish among our actions. Changing a tire or preparing a meal should require no less concentration than playing a Chopin *Étude*. Throughout his book, Pirsig encourages the amateur motorcyclist struggling with his stubborn machine: "One solution to boredom on certain routine jobs such as greasing, oil changing and tuning, is to turn them into a kind of ritual." Scrape the spark plugs, clean the battery terminals, do the dishes, darn the socks, take the garbage out. The transmutation of chores into rituals is the business of children and wise people, an elevated state denied to common mortals. But it may be enough to claim that the miracle is possible in order to make it happen.

With attention, banality disappears, meaning penetrates everywhere—every gesture, every attitude, every face. This is what happens to Malte Laurids Brigge in the streets of Paris. Every object, every event is pregnant with the weight of its own reality. Nothing is secondary, everything is equally real. The bug I squashed under the lamp is no less real *(or unreal!)* than the works of Shakespeare. "I am learning to see," writes Malte-Rilke. And then: "How can I tell what this pale green car going over the Pont-Neuf really is, or a wall poster on a group of gray houses? Everything is simplified, reduced to a few clear, true images, like the face on a portrait by Manet. And nothing is meaningless or superfluous."

This ideal seems attractive but unattainable. Deep down, we don't feel concerned. There is very little space in our "materialist" culture for this minute attention to material reality, which is a common attitude in the East. Efficiency, in our world, is left to machines. We manufacture artificial limbs of all sorts, turning the dwellers of our cities into lonely beings hooked up to countless networks. Matter is cut into small pieces, examined under microscopes; our scientists extract secrets from it, add polymers and polymorphs, draw up lists of cells and genes, and wonder at the changes in scale. From the basic proton to the lambda cell, the difference in size is inconceivable; the passage from the atomic level to the biological one is as great as the passage from one reality to another, from sleep to being awake: a leap of thought.

As for the body, it is no longer the opaque elastic container it has been since time immemorial, but a glass house, a catalog of multicolored images. Explored in its deepest corners, exposed to probes, scanners, periscopes, photographed from every angle and on every scale, manipulated, transfused, transformed into kits, into an assembly of removable parts, it seems to have handed over all its secrets. However, a tale like that told by Oliver Sacks in *A Leg to Stand On*[46] may reveal to some surgeons another aspect of their art.

Having suffered a dramatic fall in the mountains of Norway, Sacks, an outstanding neurologist, describes his accident and its medical consequences. Alone in the frozen altitudes, he injured a quadriceps and had to crawl back down to town where an emergency operation was performed. According to the surgeons, the operation was successful. But when he awoke Sacks was astonished to find in his bed a huge white object, as large as a person and extremely irritating. Distraught, he called the nurse, growing more frantic and indignant until finally, with the sheer strength of despair, he took hold of the cumbersome thing and heaved it to the floor, only to find himself on the floor next to it. When the nurse explained to him that this object was his own leg, in a plaster cast, he had great difficulty believing her. Intellectually, he was prepared to admit the truth, but it was so contrary to his experience that he could not fathom it.

"Concentrate on movement, not on the muscle," said the physiotherapist. It was to take Oliver Sacks many weeks of rehabilitation—and Mendelssohn's violin concerto—to recover the feeling in his leg and thereby the use of it: "Suddenly, with no warning, no transition whatever, my leg felt alive, and real, and mine . . . I was just turning back from the corridor to my room when the miracle happened, out of the blue, the music, the walking, the presence of my leg, all at once. And now, again, I *believed* in my leg, I *knew* how to walk...."

Elated, he discovers anew his authentic, unified body, the one in which sensation corresponds to motion and circulates unobstructed from ankle to hip and to the roots of the hair. To be present in every step means that the forward motion of one's foot, if experienced fully, embodies the whole of reality at a given time. "I had an immense feeling of welcome for my lost leg, which had now returned. My leg had come home, to its home, to me. In action my body had been broken, and only now, with the return of bodily action as a whole, did my body itself again feel like a whole."

Oliver Sacks's experience is all the more disconcerting for his emphasis on the part played by "the glorious music of Mendelssohn." He had heard it the night before on the radio, and it suddenly had gone to his head like a draught of freedom—just as he was trying to bring his dead leg forward, when it had no more will of its own than a disconnected robot. Even those who do not like Mendelssohn's concerto have to admit its outstanding melodic strength. But a song by Offenbach or Frank Sinatra might generate the same impulse. All music has to do is carry meaning for the person who hears it. Melody reestablishes continuity, joins the fragments. "It was the quintessence of life. Kant called music the 'quickening art'—animating my soul, and with it my body, so that suddenly, spontaneously, I was quickened into motion, by my own perceptive and kinetic melody.... At the instant when my body merged into action, my leg became quick and alive, my flesh became music, incarnate solid music." Sacks concludes by quoting T. S. Eliot: "One is music/as long as the music lasts."

Music is in tune with the beauty of motion, which is always akin to dancing, even if the music is silent. To enter into music is to enter oneself. The Eastern ethic prescribes what Sacks discovered: the bliss of being truly oneself, no more, no less; the bliss of being whole, legs and viscera, heart and breath, toes and bones, all of them linked, made compact, brought together by the internal flame, by vigilance, by breathing— by music. Oliver Sacks recovers his leg when he is able, thanks to the melodic line of the violin, to link it to the rest of his body. Martial arts teach the unity of the body, as shown by the constant attention given to the center, to all the centers: the center of gravity, the center of the opponent's body, the center of the target, the center of one's forehead, chest, belly, hands, fingers. There can be no balance, and therefore no strength, no harmony, without this constant locating activity.

Our schools, myths, and soap operas attach little importance to the ethics of attention to oneself. This may be why we so often have the impression of living beside ourselves, as if "real life" were passing us by. "To be present in every step" is not even a secondary aim for the bright young students of our colleges and universities. Our moral values do not include it among the goals they set forth. Our heroes may be remarkable for the accuracy or the beauty of their gestures; from Ulysses to William Tell, from King Arthur to John Wayne, the lineage of sharpshooters runs through our entire culture. We praise their courage and genius. But we stop short of inquiring into the secret of the act itself, into the skill of the Homeric archer or that of the fastest gun in the West. The efficiency of the shot is taken for granted, as a narrative artifact, a dramatic convention—Superman never misses! How he reaches this goal is of no interest. Homer doesn't tell us *how* Ulysses manages to bend his bow in front of Penelope's suitors. As in the medieval judgment of God, his success proves the truth of his words; it isn't a conquest, but an identity card.

Clint Eastwood's flawless shooting seems magical, a coincidence prone to repetition. Yet such magic is always the product of hard work. The gunman's aim attains excellence thanks to intensive training, but Westerns don't even mention this part of the game, while in Asian "soaps" it is often the very heart of the plot. In the West, excellence is an acquired privilege. In the East, it is an ascetic initiation. (However, in both worlds, only a few incorruptible heroes reach the highest level.)

In Asian traditions, it sometimes takes an entire lifetime to reach that state of consciousness which opens the way to a genuine act. Turning a handle, soldering a joint, cleaning the house—each gesture contains the entire being of the person who performs it. "No instruction manual goes into the core of things, nor deals with the essential aspect of motorcycle maintenance," writes Pirsig. "What is essential is that things be taken to heart, and not a single manual even mentions that."

Sigmund Freud said that people betray their secret feelings through the cracks in their words and gestures. The repressed unconscious sends its sibylline messages through the pores of the skin, the expression in the eyes, slips of the tongue, clumsiness, forgetfulness, gaffes, tics. Through these lapses in the continuity of experience, the very being appears naked, deprived of its protective clothing, temporarily vulnerable like an eye with no eyelid. In the kitchen I stand drying bowls: one of them slips and shatters on the floor. Why that particular bowl? I have no idea, but I do recall a break in the weaving of my thoughts, a sort of hiatus, an absence; or rather, an intrusion.

The uncontrolled gesture acts like a photographer's flash, so fast it does not allow the pupil of the eye to retract and captures the naked depths of the eyeball. Hence the color red which often appears on snapshots. This is not an optical effect, but the color of blood inside the eyeball. We ignore the color of the depths of our soul. It must be dark and shining, obscene and magnificent. If lapses reveal the darkness, accurate gestures must rescue the magnificence.

The effort to master one's gestures tends to reestablish continuity, to integrate the lapses of the unconscious into the continuum of experience. Thus a series of moves in t'ai chi ch'uan, lasting a half-hour, necessarily tends to become one single continuous gesture. Attack and parry, following each other, tend to merge, imperceptibly blending into one another without any breach in continuity. To approach this utopia one relies on the pressure sent from the tanden, widening around the lower back like a heated belt.

We are light years from this ideal and we know we will never reach it. We find some consolation in the thought that the accurate assessment of our shortcomings is in itself, as in every art, a clear sign of progress. The landscape has changed, the horizon is broader, and the voyage will prove longer than expected. However, this discouraging conclusion certifies that part of the way, however short, is behind us. Everything changes, but only change endures, as Heraclitus said. Continuity evidences the permanence of change: an insatiable divinity, it demands sacrifices and swallows them all up—imitation, repetition, effort, mental images. Whatever the story told by the sonata, it must not be interrupted from beginning to end, especially during pauses. Even the great bursts of sound, the stupefying fortissimi, are integrated by contrast into the musical discourse. Musical events find meaning through their mutual relation-ship, thanks to what they deposit in the flow of memory. With each passing brushstroke, each repetition, the narrative thins out, reduced finally to a purified state. At the limit there is nothing left but the structure, wiped clean of any story, any image. Here begins true listening.

"All that is needed is to push down the key at the right time." Ironic simplicity! All that is needed! The pianist will touch the music and the painter will stroke the mountain! But each needs a "free wrist," like that described by Shitao in a passage that seems written for pianists: "The turns of the brush must be taken in one movement, and smoothness must be born of circular movements, keeping all the while a margin for space. The final brushstrokes must be clear-cut, and the attacks crisp. One must also be skilled with circular or angular shapes, straight lines and curves, rising and falling lines; the brush goes left, right, in relief, in a hollow, abrupt and resolved, it stops short, lengthens at a slant; at times it rushes like water down into the depths, at times it bursts up like a flame, always naturally, without the slightest strain."

For the pianist, each finger is a free wrist. As are the forearms, of course, and the shoulders, and the back.... To the practitioner of martial arts, the entire body is a free wrist. From the motorcyclist's perspective, the free wrist is a smooth curve on the road.

XXIII

Eventually, the camera zooms. The more you slow down, the closer the landscape appears. (As Stravinsky said, music is a moving landscape.) At this distance, my Bach fugue is but a field of ruins destroyed by earthquakes and avalanches. Collapsing gamuts create jolts in the continuity of the storytelling. My fingers are devoid of the lovely energy that stems from the awareness of the right aim, of the open path. What? Months of practice, almost lost! Flown away! Hours of passionate, minute, stubborn trying! And now, there is nothing left but shreds, frayed clouds of music. Yet a few bubbles of tenderness survive in this chaos, spirals of pleasure rescued from time's erosion.

Herrigel's master instructed: "Practice, constantly repeat what has already been repeated." Such is the price of rebuilding, in piano playing as in archery. In its deep layers, memory of a musical work or of a kata differs radically from the conscious guide marks which serve as necessary signposts: here an E-flat for the left hand, there the form "hands of clouds." Acquired automatisms serve as a mnemonic ferment in the rich soil of the gesture, which grows more and more confident the deeper its roots reach down to its well-hidden, thus unshakable, foundations. The old house will not be restored but replaced by a new one just like it. But the new construction is then adorned with new colors, unexpected resonances. Novelty comes only from delving deeper into the score, bringing its latent possibilities to fruition.

Pianists never know when the truth of the score will begin to coincide with their own. It comes without warning. Beneath the surface a world appears. Underwater flowers open their corollas. The ocean floor becomes visible: the spine, the inward structure, the combination of themes, the series of modulations. In this Brahms intermezzo, the second of the Opus 117, all it takes is two notes— a C stepping in to resolve a B-flat—to open up an entire harmonic universe. I knew it already, but this time I try insisting a bit more, drawing it out, listening to the vibration of the B-flat until it ends, following the curve of the sound as it fades out and gives in to the resolving C. The true nature of the B-flat makes itself heard at last: a heralding angel.

"After executing your hold, if you make the motion of emptying a glass of *sake,* your opponent will hang by the wrist like a dishrag." Kenji Tokitsu quotes this sentence from the jujitsu master Kubota to show the necessity of avoiding stagnation: "When you seize your adversary's wrist your hand must not remain blocked, not even for a short while. After a stagnation, you would no longer be able to exert the right pressure with the root of your index finger and you would lose the efficiency of your grip. Stagnation is the illness of the martial arts."[47] A gesture is either continuous or it simply doesn't exist.

How not to forget my left wrist when concentrating on the motion of my right leg and the loop it must form? The right foot comes from behind, having carried, on the back of its heel, an imaginary cannonball; it pauses in a protective position in front of the slightly bent, very stable left knee, then progresses forward again, and starts descending toward the ground, braking softly, as if separated from the floor by an invisible cushion, gradually removing space between the sole of the foot and the floor.

The attention I give to the motion of this leg (in fact, a stylized kick) should not lead me to neglect what is happening elsewhere (what "I" am doing with the rest of my body) at the same infinitely (unbearably!) slow rhythm. Actually, my entire body is slowly twisting in a long spiral toward the left. The spine expands, massaging the muscles of the left flank and stretching the pelvis; meanwhile, subtly linked to my right leg through the center of my body, my left arm rises toward the southwest like a large bird struggling against the wind. My hand is open wide around the central void of the palm (exactly sized to fit the invisible apple which beginning pianists are given to hold, in order build up the strong muscular architecture without which their best intentions fall apart); the index finger and the thumb are spread facing each other, pincer-like: this is the *tiger's jaw*. The left arm pursues its unceasing curve, brushes by the ear in its slow progression, bringing everything forward, from the fingertips to the shoulder and back, toward the (imaginary) opponent's center, gently reversing the general spiral while the center of gravity slowly shifts onto the right leg.

The right arm also follows the moving twist. Sustained by the shoulder which guides it from a distance, linked by intention to the still advancing right leg, it rises forward like an offering, then like a flame, and finally turns on itself to retreat palm downwards (with the sensation of pulling backward the entire space of the dojo, including the wall). It duly arrives where the left arm used to be: the spiral is reversed. Without a break, imperceptibly, the movement has started again in the opposite direction, in a loop. The right leg is doing the left leg's previous task, its knee firmly planted, while the left foot starts on its way, weighing its cannonball....

Absorbed by the tension of the right foot and the fullness it has been sending through my legs and belly, I forget my left arm, blocked in flight like a paralyzed bird. Bad! Very bad! Stagnation! My descending right foot forgets to squeeze the empty space above the ground like an air bag. Bad! Very bad! Empty! Busy with all the information I must combine, I forget to breathe deeply, which instantly gives my gestures a jerky, crude quality. General stagnation.

But how can we think of all these things? In any case, how can we think of several things at once? Is it even conceivable? To make it possible, no doubt all these things must be made into one, woven into the same fabric as various aspects of a unique reality. In t'ai chi ch'uan, as in a fugue with several voices, each strand is as present and important as the others, even if they belong to different levels. Pianissimo is not by nature less present, less active, than forte. Who would dare to assert that the background of a Renaissance painting is less important than the angelic faces in the foreground? Every aspect of an art form deserves attention, care, understanding, consideration, sympathy. In return, it bestows the special delight it is designed to give. The right ankle should not forget the left wrist: they are linked to the same control tower, our old friend the tanden.

The pianist may happen to be absent-minded. In the middle of a piece, during a few notes, a few bars, he forgets what he is playing and thinks of something else. If this goes on for too long, the music becomes a shade mechanical and loses the listener. (Often, the listener does not know why he has started to daydream instead of listening.) Musical stagnation.

Four voices in a fugue for one listener, one consciousness. How to give them the attention they require? How not to neglect the alto, the in-between voice, except when it calls for attention by voicing the theme? How to avoid slackening the dramatic tension during transitions (the last thing one attends to, when there is really no other choice)? Bad! Very bad!

In t'ai chi ch'uan, transitions also tend to get little attention, at least in the beginning. If they are botched, it means one's approach to continuity is still incomplete: each move is being treated as a separate entity. The beginner's vision does not yet possess the retinal persistence that comes with memory; he imagines successive postures. In the intervals, the transitions are pushed aside, forgotten. On the contrary, when transitions do begin to exist, to shape up, they make a powerful contribution to the continuity of the whole. Like J. S. Bach's fugues, t'ai chi ch'uan is both melodic and harmonic, a combination of parts forming a whole, diverse and unified. The melody of t'ai chi ch'uan is the trail of the gesture displayed into open space. Its harmony is the sensation it carries, which in turn expands consciousness. Add the entire parade of lateral thoughts, the color of the wooden floor, the smell and density of the air. All this melts into the present time and makes it different from any other moment of time.

The beautiful gesture embodies unity of time, place, and action. A magnificent classic.

XXIV

What about those days that get off to a bad start, full of fading impulses and lackluster thoughts, bleak stretches of time where one's inner chaos makes the world cottony, where nothing falls in place, where nothing gets done? Clumsiness begins to snowball, objects rebel and escape: I lose my keys, spill my coffee, forget to turn off the gas, can no longer play that Chopin *Étude* I have been working on for such a long time, forget a friend waiting at the nearby café. A sense of urgency makes me spin off into vacuity like a top with a twisted axis. On days like this, thoughts keep wandering off. Heating the coffee reminds me of a call I should make. Talking on the phone, I think of the letter I have put off writing. As I switch on the Mac, I begin to worry about that passage in the Beethoven sonata, the one I just can't get right....

I sit down at the piano—the coffee is warm, the letter can wait—and open Bach's *Fantasia and Fugue in G minor*, an old torn score, victim of zealous page-turnings. I decide to play the theme, just to see how it sounds. I get caught up in the exhilarating whirl, right up to the *grandes orgues* of the end. An hour goes by, two hours. I still have to pay the bills and do the shopping. Guilt demands to be fed; once sated, it lets go.

On these blurry days, confused gestures preside over their own meaningless succession. Spurts of energy wither and ring hollow. Time seems full of holes, threadbare, impossible to mend. Gaps in consciousness attract things, causing cups to fall, or keys, wallets, and toothbrushes to disappear. When these mishaps occur in too rapid succession, the day is shot. Write it off, you need a break. Go to the corner café for a cappuccino.

It is meaning itself that is leaking through these unraveling gestures, like a drop of water from a leaky tap. Take the subway, tidy up the house, make a phone call, water the plants in the window boxes. These gestures or others, what is the difference? What is the use, anyway, and for whom? Words themselves seem to panic. How to distinguish shame from boredom? Writing a single sentence means that something else is not getting done. Why say this instead of that? Silt rises from the pond. A chaotic alphabet invades the scene like a cloud of locusts, and strips it bare. After that, even the silence is feverish. What can a gesture do about it? Nothing. Everything.

Nothing! The gesture is hidden, weakened, unavailable. Indifference and sloth cover everything up. The body sprawls, the spirit wallows. The world is intensely absurd, repulsive. Expectations, tamed by experience, fall into lethargy. At times like this, sleep it out if you can. *When the world is upside down, just hail the proud figure of the curving seahorse lighting up the opaque mass of the ocean.*

Everything! The gesture is all-powerful. It does not disappear. A mobile sculpture, a silent score, it resides in the deepest recesses of memory. Once registered there, it sets to work (in what neurons, chemical transmitters, material archives?). Unrelenting, efficient, it engraves its messages in the underground, in the uncanny labyrinths of being, untroubled by whatever moods may rage on the surface. Its only substance is the weight of time. After a fortnight of fasting from the piano, there it is, still foggy from the depths, yet ready for use. Surprise! Progress has been made. When the gesture at last surfaces again, cleansed, enlarged, bursting with fresh meaning, it dominates the landscape with its simple presence. Chaos evaporates, shapes come into focus. Later on, of course, you return to earth and have to go back to the previous level, start working again—repeat, repeat, repeat, repeat. Gesture is a "crystal of historical memory."[48]

XXV

"You say you embrace. Are you sure of it?" What an insolent question! Is it metaphysical, material? What *is* the difference? What reality does the physical body give to love? Where lies the truth, *if not in the rush of passion through the atoms of your open arms?* Between an absent-minded stroke and a loving embrace, the distance is the same as that between a daily gesture made consciously and the involuntary trembling of hands afflicted with Parkinson's disease.

In the Sixties, as a neurologist at Mount Carmel Hospital in New York, Oliver Sacks decided to experiment on patients who had been bedridden for over half a century, using a new drug, L-Dopa, which had a dramatic effect on sufferers of Parkinson's disease. These patients, called post-encephalitic, were survivors of the major epidemic of *encephalitis lethargica* (sleeping sickness) which raged during the winter of 1916–1917 and killed or severely handicapped nearly 10 million people worldwide before disappearing in 1927, as mysteriously as it had appeared. These unfortunate survivors, forgotten in the wards of Mount Carmel, were reduced to a state of living death, extinguished volcanoes. "They did not give the impression of being alive, nor did they feel alive; they were as insubstantial as ghosts, and as passive as zombies."[49]

The effect of L-Dopa was extraordinary, like Prince Charming's kiss on Sleeping Beauty's lips. Within a few days, after fifty years of sleep, "about half an hour after receiving her morning gram of

L-Dopa, Hester Y. suddenly jumped to her feet, and before incredulous eyes started walking back and forth. 'What do you think of that, eh?' she exclaimed in a loud, excited voice. 'What do you think of that?'" One after the other, as if torn from a spell, the post-encephalitic patients awoke, began to talk, walk, write, and sing songs from before the First World War, apparently intact and unaware of the timespan of their illness. Miracle followed miracle, day after day, before the amazed staff.

In *Awakenings*, Oliver Sacks tells this incredible story with unceasing astonishment and love. Alas, the fairytale inexorably became a nightmare. The drug, while awakening the brain, brought to light destroyed zones and induced dramatic side effects. Everything happened as if the return to movement after an intoxicating passage through ordinary time was followed by a devastating acceleration. The lethargic patients became maniacs, tormented by tics. Some were seized by chorea, a sort of involuntary dance where "motions would suddenly appear, without effort or warning, totally unpredictably." There are, explains Oliver Sacks, neurological links, "interconversions," between the rigidity of Parkinson's disease or post-encephalitis and the rag-doll agitation of chorea, between excess lethargy and excess mobility—just as it seems that there exist, in the heart of the Sahara desert, places where the thermometer reaches 120°F during the day only to plunge at night to well below freezing.

Oliver Sacks' books are filled with the tangible paradoxes he encountered in plumbing the reality

behind neurological disturbances. The extravagant
fits of "festination" are no less morbid than the
immobility which precedes them. Sacks writes
about Hester Y: "Completely motionless and sub-
merged for over twenty years, she had surfaced
and shot into the air like a cork released from a
great depth." Euphoria! Freedom! "She made me
think of prisoners released from jail; I thought of
children released from school; I thought of spring
awakenings after winter sleeps; I thought of the
Sleeping Beauty; and I also thought, with some
foreboding, of catatonics, suddenly frenzied."
Unfortunately, liberty regained soon gave way to
an inverted form of slavery. Before long the film
had picked up speed and Hester Y. was dashing
off like a racehorse gone berserk. "My colleagues,
looking at a film of Mrs. Y. which I took at this
time, insisted the projector was running too fast. . . .
I have known a number of Olympic athletes, but
Mrs. Y. could have beaten them all in terms of
reaction-time; under other circumstances she could
have been the fastest gun in the West."

Before long tics began to appear, the onset of
torture. In her journal, written at full speed, she
wonders if she is being held in a concentration
camp. "These tics affect every aspect of action and
behavior, and one may often perceive a dozen or
two proceeding *simultaneously,* each one apparently
autonomous, in complete functional isolation
from one another." This last sentence holds the
key to the symptom. Pathology is dispersion.
Inversely, the beauty of a gesture lies in the way
it ties everything together.

The scattered gestures of patients like Hester Y. reveal an absence of connection between them, an absence of control indicating the seriousness of the crisis as well as its ontological depth. This is why compulsive movements inspire in us infinite compassion. We tend to think that terminally bed-ridden people do not suffer; at least their pain is diffuse, misty, unconscious. But those who suffer from tics, abandoned without recourse to their own internal anarchy! Like the fellow in my neighbor-hood, whose leg describes a corkscrew motion when he raises his hand to an nonexistent hat; he waves a greeting then pulls up straight, petting all the while an imaginary dog. It takes him several minutes to get his wallet out of his pocket. People watch, laughing. Then he starts all over again.

Perhaps the most beautiful passage in Rilke (apart from the *Duino Elegies*) is the one in *The Notebooks of Malte Laurids Brigge* in which he describes the secret solidarity he feels towards a man beleaguered with tics. The scene takes place in the lower part of the Boulevard Saint Michel, near the Seine: "From that moment I was bound to him. I understood that this hopping impulse was wandering about his body, trying to break out here and there. I understood why he was afraid of people, and I myself began cautiously to test whether passers-by noticed anything. A cold stab went through my back when his legs suddenly gave a slight, jerking spasm, but no one saw it, and I thought out the plan of stumbling myself a little in case anyone began to notice. That would certainly be one way of making the curious believe that some small, inconspicuous obstacle really had been lying in the road, on which both of us had happened to tread." I'm tempted to quote the entire text. Such incredible compassion testifies to Rilke's greatness on that day.

Our gestures distinguish us as surely as our faces or clothes. But in the wincing mask of a face shaken by involuntary tics, nothing personal can show. The one who suffers disappears behind his tics—phantom gestures, cut off from their source. The pity we feel for these beings enslaved by their gestures arises from our instinctive knowledge of the closeness between spirit and motion. If his gestures are chaotic, what a mess his soul must be.

Seymour L., another post-encephalitic treated with L-Dopa, was walking along the corridor, when he suddenly began to run like a madman, and burst into Sacks's office to complain furiously: "Why the hell do they leave an enormous hole in the middle of the corridor?" He had suddenly seen a huge declivity and started "normally" to run, in a logical effort to regain his balance. "It was *because* it dipped that I was forced into a run. You'd do the same if you felt the ground falling out, from under your feet." In this case a normal reaction responds to an abnormal perception. The breach is no longer between the gesture and its command but between exterior reality and his internal perception. Yet the result is the same: tragedy.

As for Miron V., his story is as disturbing as *An Incident at Owl Creek*. Sacks writes, "I noted above that he often seemed to sit, absolutely immobile, for fifteen hours at a stretch, but this is not wholly correct. I would sometimes see him in the morning, silhouetted against a frosted-glass door, with his right hand apparently motionless a few inches from his knee. I might catch sight of him later, towards the middle of the day, with his hand stuck halfway to his nose. Then, a couple of hours later, his hand would be 'frozen' on his glasses or his nose. I assumed that these were meaningless akinetic poses, and it was only much later, when he was awakened and accelerated by L-Dopa, that the almost incredible truth came out. I remembered his strange 'frozen poses,' and mentioned them to him.

"'What do you mean, "frozen poses?"' he exclaimed. 'I was merely scratching my nose!'

"'But Miron, this just isn't possible. Are you telling me that what I saw as frozen poses was your hand in transit to your nose?'

"'It sounds crazy,' he reflected, 'and scary too. To me they were just normal movements, it just took a second. Are you saying it took me *hours* instead of *seconds* to scratch my nose?'

"I didn't know what to answer. I was as perplexed as he was. It did, indeed, sound perfectly absurd. However, I had countless photos of Miron in his erect pose, silhouetted against the door. I put together thirty of them, taken in the course of one day, made cinephoto-size reductions, and ran them through a projector at sixteen frames a second. Now, incredibly, I saw that the 'impossible' was true; . . . The succession of 'poses' did, in fact, form a contin-uous action. He was, indeed, just scratching his nose, *ten thousand times more slowly than normal*."

How ironic to reflect that Miron V.'s patho-
logical slowness achieves, albeit involuntarily, an
ideal of t'ai chi ch'uan, the ability to slow one's
movement to the extremes of time, to attain a
kind of temporal pianissimo (its reverse side, its
aim, its reward being the ability to release strength
with a swift thrust). In this expanded perception
of time, motion tends toward the slowness of a
clock's minute hand, toward the imperceptible
pace of plants growing.

Miron V.'s experience is but a dramatic caricature
of the continuous distortions in our perception
of time. Thanks to Miron V., Hester Y., Seymour
L., and all the other characters of Sacks' true-life
neurological account, we learn that duration is a
totally subjective and incommensurable phenom-
enon. Fortunately we are not faced with such
terrifying temporal chasms, but we are by no means
free of the magical effects of illusion. Our existence
is punctuated by minute breaks, extensions, skips,
accelerations, abrupt halts.

Slowness and speed are no less relative than
love and hate. And just as the word springs from
silence, the gesture is rooted in stillness. That is
why the ri tsu zen aims at nourishing the roots,
consolidating the foundations. "In the practice
of standing meditation, the exponent attempts to
imagine different movements of technique and
of combat situation, without actually moving.
Perfecting the sensations inherent to motion draws
him nearer to the essence of technique. From there
emerges one of the paradoxes of Budo: fast is not
as good as slow, slow is not as good as still. To find

true motion one must immerse oneself in immobility, and this is the meaning of the exercise of standing zen," says Kenji Tokitsu.

Between the immobility of Miron V., pure stagnation, and that of a t'ai chi master, potential motion, the distance is the same as from the ocean floor to the mountaintops.

Hölderlin. Thirty-six years of childhood and genius, thirty-seven years of discord and insanity. A life broken down in the middle along the length of time. The year of the break: 1806, followed by eons of boredom and suffering, neither death nor life, with an out-of-tune piano. Through the window, the prince of poets could see a landscape as clear as a child's drawing.

At the time of his madness, Bettina von Arnim visited him in the carpenter Zimmer's room. Then she wrote: "The Princess of Homburg has given him a grand piano, and he has cut the strings, but not all of them, so that some of the keys still play, and he improvises on them. This piano, from which he himself has torn the strings, is the image of his soul."[50]

XXVI

"Who fails to wonder at the chameleon, which
we are?" According to Pico de la Mirandola, it is
man's *plasticity* which makes him human, his
talent for metamorphosis, which is the result of
his late appearance in the universe.[51] When the
Creator finished his work, he had the idea of making
man. But all the seats were taken. "Every place
was full, every thing had already been distributed
among the superior, intermediate and inferior
orders." There was nothing left in stock, no more
shapes, no more species. Annoyed, God solved
the problem by deciding to create the Man without
Qualities (as Robert Musil would say): "The perfect
artisan finally decided that, as he could not give
anything specific to man, he would make him the
common ground for everything which was specific
to each creature." This is why man is part angel,
part beast. Wise and foolish, child and elder, lion
and mosquito, cloud and tempest, ignoble and
sublime, he dwells in all universes, wanders along
every path. His freedom gives him access to all
parts of Creation. Thus God creates man and says
to him: "I have given you neither fixed abode, nor
specific face, nor any particular gift, in order that
you may desire, conquer and possess your abode,
face and gifts."

This is precisely what Confucius says in a famous
maxim: "The man of virtue is not a utensil." This
means, according to Pierre Ryckmans, that "human
abilities are not confined within the exclusive
limitations of a certain specialized usage, and that,

unlike a pot, human receptivity is not limited to a given capacity or specific content." As a limitless receptacle, the human being is his own potter. He has no other choice than to forge himself at each moment of his life, as an artist shapes his work. What allows him to create himself is his ability to transform himself. His words and gestures entwined are his tools. They serve to give and to receive. Such a creature can endure everything, without losing its ability to enjoy all the given worlds. But everything is left up to him. It is his responsibility to shape his outlines, to complete the sketch, to become this particular person, in this time and place. It's up to him to find his way among possibilities, to mold chaos, to locate the essential in a formless object.

A story about Rodin tells how he took delivery one morning of a huge block of marble. The son of the concierge, a boy of twelve, was watching with wide eyes. It was the day before the start of the summer holiday. In September, the boy returned from his vacation and fell awestruck before the superb white horse standing in the atelier in place of the marble block. Then he asked the sculptor: "How did you know there was a horse hiding in there?" Do we know how to find the white steed prancing in our thoughts, with its mane flying in the wind?

The chameleon-man is set in the center of the world, and he holds all the keys. "In every child who is born, the Father has planted all kinds of seeds, germs of all species of life." It is up to the child to make the seeds bear fruits, to bring them into existence, to find a direction in the maze of his destiny. Man alone can visit all worlds, become demon or cherub. "Man is a living being of a varied, multiform and fickle nature."

Pico de la Mirandola's intuition echoes the modern distinction between the instinct of animals, which leaves them only an infinitesimal space for decisions, and the infinite range of possibilities open to the human being, whose instinct is reduced to a tiny portion. The flexibility of the program accounts for the great diversity in our modes of being. Among those gifts we receive at birth, how many remain unexploited, unknown, undreamed of? How many threads are cut in the tapestry? How many secret renunciations go into the building of a life?

What would Mozart have become in a world without harpsichords or written scores, without Leopold? How many undiscovered geniuses, silenced at birth, were born and lived their life in the dark ages preceding Homer and Pericles? In the obscurity of our unrealized futures we harbor a host of impossible destinies: ship's captain, dancer, philosopher. Our random choices only take shape into a story under the pressure of events, thanks to the logic of language. Most often, we feel that we are drifting aimlessly on the surface of time. To keep on track, we must really want to. But why are we so surprised when we find out that others navigate differently?

Not a day goes by without a new experience making us aware of other possible outlooks on things. Yet all humans tread on the same earth and watch the same clouds that have been there for so long. And all have speech in common, but not language, which is the source of many a tragedy. Gestures, like music, transcend the curse of the Tower of Babel. They are universal languages and can be understood by all. If motion is analogous to music, one can imagine that deaf people, apparently deprived of music, still have access to it through sign language, rhythm, expression, vocabulary, phrasing, modulations. Even though the same words can be used to describe them, motion and music are not identical; but they are Siamese twins.

The price the chameleon-man has to pay for his freedom is his difficulty in simply being content to be himself. We are all akin to Franz Kafka's Gregor Samsa, part scarab, part firefly. Through his gestures, the "plastic" man is the active object of perpetual molting. Each of his gestures changes him, leaves its mark on him, its invisible trace. They accumulate and carve their wrinkles, as sea foam wears away the millennial rocks on the cliff. We brag of being able to fashion our gestures, but it is our gestures that sculpt us. We are the raw material of their creation. As the photographer Selgado said, "the man who works ends up resembling his product."

Nature hates immobility. No less than language, but in a deeper, more archaic way, our gestures link us to our ancestors and, if we trace our way back through the chain of species, to the origins of life. The first multicellular organisms appeared in the Cambrian era, 570 million years ago, and were equipped for all kinds of movement.[52]

Along with the names of things, our parents handed down to us a particular way of touching, of looking, of kissing. No less than words (but perhaps we should consider them a different kind of words), gestures are at the basis of our relationships with others. The gestures of love link us, do they not, to the emotions of our ancestors, who loved each other in order to enable us to do the same. It is also possible to foresee that our descendants will in their embraces encounter an aftertaste of what was once our paradise, or our hell.

The chameleon-man can become what he wills. He can hew himself from the huge block of marble containing the white horse of his dreams, just as music reveals silence by weaving it into its fabric. Music differs from noise by uniting silence and sound. Shaping their encounter, it gives them life. We all know that beautiful silence contains music. One day in the dojo, Kenji Tokitsu says: "Don't listen to the sounds up close but only to the murmur of the cars on the boulevard." The boulevard is a hundred yards away. Impossible! However, instead of fading away, the noises of the building become unusually sharp—the faucet, the dog, the bird, my neighbor's breathing, my own heartbeat. Suddenly, what a racket in the large silent room! Only once we have been through the entire catalog of nearby sounds can we dismiss them and direct our attention to the faraway rumble of the city revolving around the fixed point of our silent bodies. "Heaven is above the roof, so blue, so calm ..." said Verlaine, or was it Schubert?

And the caress, the queen of gestures? Have we forgotten her? Is her tiny light threatened by the low level of our desires? Through the freezing void separating our lone selves she projects her antennae, builds her bridges, lightens the day. The caress beckons to all the other gestures, and they turn to her as plants to the sun. She slips through skin and viscera to reach the soul, along secret paths which she alone knows. In her wake, there's music and laughter, blinking lights, whispers in the darkness.

Plodding and patient or fleeting and weightless, the caress celebrates limits. It is, says the philosopher Emmanuel Levinas, "a state of being in which one conscience in contact with another goes beyond that contact."[53] The caress questions the other person in that person's intimate reality, that is, life experience. Is not love precisely that ability to recognize what the other person is feeling and to incorporate this knowledge into our actions and gestures? That is why the caress possesses all powers, at least when it beats with the pulse and truth of desire. It can bring peace, laughter, defeat, pleasure, or tears, whatever. It diffuses delight and caprice throughout the skin, right into the roots of being. "It does not know what it seeks," continues Levinas. The caress gropes its way through the dark and feeds upon the pleasure it gives to light up the world.

Alas, in its sincere, fresh version it is frowned on by our broken world. We keep shattering things—truces, ties, habits. In this general breakdown the caress, which unites and connects, seems obsolete and negligible. It appears and fades like the poppy, which wilts as soon as it is picked. This is a queen with no throne. Above all, beware of counterfeits! Phony caresses are the weeds of secret gardens. The fading fingers of the sated lover, absentmindedly patting two square inches of skin. Empty gestures are declarations of indifference.

The clatter of forks has faded away, but to them the atmosphere in the restaurant, permeated with smells of frying, seems to vibrate with tenderness. Their reflection can be seen in the window, two blurred heads leaning close. For hours they have been talking, gazing fondly at each other.

What time did the event take place? She couldn't say. Around ten-twenty (or ten twenty-two — even a neutron clock couldn't capture that precise moment), without warning, he reached over to her cheek and bound through a wide stroke her beating temple to the soft expanse of her chest.

The beauty of the gesture resides in the smile it arouses. It is directed to the other person, not as an onlooker but as a conscious being, sensitive to grace and worthy of love. It bestows an experience and testifies that harmony is possible. Now we come to the main point. The "beautiful gesture" is not only a splendid curve but an act of generosity, a way for the chameleon-man to explore the mysterious world of others. Making a beautiful gesture, giving one's coat, or life, pretending to stumble on the Boulevard Saint Michel—these are gifts of no return. The beautiful gesture is not to be valued for its largesse, nor the sacrifice it entails, nor the personality of the beneficiary. By nature, it is disinterested. As Rabbénou Yona has written: "Pure generosity is greater than charity, because it cares equally for the rich and the poor, whereas charity is meant only for the poor. Pure generosity applies to the body of man as well as to his possessions, whereas charity applies only to his possessions. Thanks to his inclination towards generosity, the human being pleases the Eternal. That is why the world was created, to give generosity a place in which it can be realized."[54]

Paris, January 1994.

Notes

In many instances, I give my own translations of material cited from French editions of works that also exist or were originally published in English. Wherever possible, I have provided the publication information on the English language editions so that the reader may easily find these titles.

1. Shitao, *Propos sur la peinture du moine Citrouille-Amère*. Translated from the Chinese and annotated (admirably) by Pierre Ryckmans. (Paris: Hermann, 1984). One of the great classics of Chinese aesthetics.

2. T'ai chi ch'uan, originally a Chinese martial art, is often practiced today, even in China, for purely aesthetic purposes, like dance or yoga. Research done by Kenji Tokitsu, based on Japanese karate, attempts to recreate, through the martial aspect of t'ai chi ch'uan, its original aim: efficiency. The meaning of the sequence of gestures only becomes apparent in relation to the opponent. Without this reality test, t'ai chi ch'uan remains a beautiful form devoid of its deeper meaning.

3. Japanese term for a room used for the practice of various disciplines, from martial arts to meditation.

4. A Japanese term meaning "standing Zen." A product of Chinese Ch'an Buddhism, Zen is both a way of perceiving the world and a meditative discipline. Meditation is not limited to a motionless posture, but also takes place during a sequence of movements following established rules, or indeed during all activities in one's daily life.

5. See Eugen Herrigel, *Zen in the Art of Archery*. Introduction by Daisetz T. Suzuki (New York, Pantheon Books, 1953). This little book by the German philosopher tells of his initiation into archery with a Japanese master. Quoted text is my translation from the French edition, *L'art chevaleresque de tir à l'arc* (Paris: Dervy, 1987).

6. The sequences of moves in t'ai chi ch'uan taught in the school of Kenji Tokitsu (called "*Shaolin mon*," which means "the gateway of Shaolin") are, for the most part, interpretations of forms that originated at the renowned Shaolin temple in China where t'ai chi ch'uan was invented.

7. Henri Atlan, "La mémoire du rite: métaphore de fécondation," in *Mémoire et Histoire*. Edited by Jean Halperein and Georges Levitee (Paris: Denoël, 1986).

8. See Robert Pirsig, *Zen and the Art of Motorcycle Maintenance: An Inquiry into Values* (New York: Morrow, 1974). Quoted text is my translation from the French edition, *Traité du zen et l'entretien des motocyclettes* (Paris: Le Seuil, 1984).

9. See Jean Bottero, *Mésopotamie. L'Ecriture, la Raison et les Dieux* (Paris: Éditions Gallimard, 1987).

10. See Rainer Maria Rilke, *Rodin.* Translated by Robert Firmage (Salt Lake City, Utah: Peregrine Smith, 1979). Quoted text is my translation from the French edition, *Auguste Rodin, Première partie*, in *Oeuvres en prose* (Paris: Éditions Gallimard, Collection la Pleiade, 1993).

11. Boris Cyrulnik, "Pluriel," in *Mémoires de singe et paroles d'homme* (Paris: Hachette, 1983).

12. A Japanese term denoting a series of codified moves which imitate combat in a cryptic form.

13. Quoted by Giorgio Agamben in "Revue de Cinéma," *Trafic*, No. 1, Winter 1991 (Paris, Éditions P.O.L.), p. 31.

14. Agamben, *Trafic*, p. 34.

15. See Jacques Drillon, *Charles d'Orléans ou le génie mélancolique.* (Paris: Lattès, 1993).

16. Vladimir Jankelevitch, *De la musique au silence. Liszt et la rhapsodie* (Paris: Plon, 1979), p. 94.

17. Kenji Tokitsu, *Étude sur le rôle et les transformations de la culture traditionnelle dans la société contemporaine japonaise*, unpublished doctoral thesis, 1993.

18. Jankelevitch, p. 100.

19. Quoted in Kenji Tokitsu, "Points," *Voie du karaté: Pour une théorie des arts martiaux japonais* (Paris: Le Seuil, 1979), p. 142.

20. Rainer Maria Rilke, "Du Monde entier," in *Correspondance avec Lou Andreas Salome* (Paris: Gallimard, 1985).

21. "Sun, severed neck." Apollinaire, "Zone," in *Alcools.* (The first line reads: *"Bergère, ô Tour Eiffel, le troupeau des ponts bêle ce matin...."*)

22. Stephane Mosès, *L'Ange de l'Histoire. Essai sur Rosenzweig, Benjamin et Scholem* (Paris: Le Seuil, 1992), p. 116.

23. Walter Benjamin, cited in Mosès, *L'Ange de l'Histoire.*

24. See Miyamoto Musashi, *A Book of Five Rings*. Translated by Victor Harris (New York: The Overlook Press, 1974).

25. Tokitsu, *Étude sur le rôle et les transformations de la culture traditionnelle dans la société contemporaine japonaise.*

26. Jacques Derrida, *De l'esprit. Heidegger et la question* (Paris: Galilée, 1987), p. 165.

27. See Josef Hayim Yerushalmi, *Zakhor. Jewish History and Jewish Memory* (Seattle: University of Washington Press, 1982).

28. See Pirsig, *Zen and the Art of Motorcycle Maintenance.*

29. Expression used by Nietzsche in reference to Baudelaire, as quoted by Stéphane Mosès in *L'Ange de l'Histoire*, p. 122.

30. See Robert Musil, *The Man Without Qualities*. Translated by Sophie Wilkins (New York: Knopf, 1995).

31. "It is found again/.../It is the sea gone/with the sun." Rimbaud, in "3. L'Eternité," from the poem *Fêtes de la Patience.*

32. See John Chadwick, *The Decipherment of Linear B* (London: Cambridge University Press, 1958; Second edition, 1967).

33. See Rainer Maria Rilke, *The Notebooks of Malte Laurids Brigge*, translated by M. D. Herder Norton (New York: W. W. Norton, 1949).

34. See Herrigel, *Zen and the Art of Archery.*

35. Heinrich von Kleist, *Sur le théâtre de marionnettes* (Paris: Mille et Une Nuits, 1993).

36. Stella Baruk, *C'est à dire, en mathématiques ou ailleurs* (Paris: Le Seuil, 1994).

37. Joseph Roth, *Job: The Story of a Simple Man*. Translated by Dorothy Thompson (New York: Viking, 1931).

38. Quoted by Kenji Tokitsu in reference to Miyamoto Musashi, in *Voie du karaté: Pour une théorie des arts martiaux japonais.*

39. See Sigmund Freud, *Delusion and Dream: An Interpretation in the Light of Psychoanalysis of Gradiva, a novel, by Wilhelm Jensen,* preceded by *Gradiva* by Wilhelm Jensen (New York: Moffat, Yard, 1917).

40. "Un rêve de pierre," the title (borrowed from a phrase of Baudelaire) of an article by Isi Beller in *Gradiva, Tel Quel* (Paris: Le Seuil, 1991).

41. As did Baudelaire before him, in his poem *A une passante:* "La rue assourdissante autour de moi hurlait./Longue, mince, en grand deuil, douleur majestueuse,/Une femme

passa, d'une main fastueuse/Soulevant, balançant le feston et l'ourlet...." ("The deafening street around me shouted./Tall and slender in her mourning dress, majestic pain,/A woman passed by, her sumptuous hand/Raising, swirling the festoon and the hem....")

42. Georges Didi-Huberman, *Invention de l'hystérie. Charcot et l'iconographie photographique de la Salpêtrière* (Paris: Macula, 1982).

43. My interpretation of this passage from the Second Elegy. See Rainer Maria Rilke, *Duino Elegies.* Translated by J. B. Leishman and Stephen Spender (New York: W. W. Norton, 1939).

44. Tokitsu, *Voie du karaté: Pour une théorie des arts martiaux japonais,* p. 5.

45. *L'amour n'est pas aimé,* title of a novel by Hector Bianciotti (Paris: Éditions Gallimard, 1982).

46. See Oliver Sacks, *A Leg to Stand On* (New York: Summit Books, 1984). Quoted text is my translation from the French edition, *Sur Une Jambe* (Paris: Le Seuil, 1987).

47. Tokitsu, *Voie du karaté: Pour une théorie des arts martiaux japonais.*

48. Agamben, *Trafic.*

49. See Oliver Sacks, *Awakenings* (New York: Dutton, 1983). Quoted text is my translation from the French edition, *Cinquante ans de sommeie* (Paris: Le Seuil, 1987).

50. Quoted in *Les romantiques allemands,* edited by Armel Guerne (Paris: Desclée de Brouwer), p. 73.

51. Pico de la Mirandola, *De la dignité de l'homme,* in *Oeuvres philosophiques* (Paris: P.U.F., 1993), p. 9.

52. See Stephen J. Gould, *Wonderful Life: The Burgess Shale and Nature of History* (New York: W. W. Norton, 1989).

53. Emmanuel Levinas, quoted by Marc-Alain Ouaknin in *Méditations érotiques. Essai sur Emmanuel Levinas* (Paris: Balland, 1992), p. 132.

54. Moise Maimonide, Rachi, Rabbénou Yona, the Maharal of Prague, Rabbi Hayim of Volozhyn, in *Commentaires du Traité des pères (Pirqé avot)* (Paris: Verdier, 1990), p. 52.